FRANCISCO DE MIRANDA: EXILE AND ENLIGHTENMENT

Institute for the Study of the Americas History Series

This series succeeds the Nineteenth-Century Latin America Series published by the former Institute of Latin American Studies, University of London. The Institute for the Study of the Americas was established in August 2004 as a result of a merger between the Institute of Latin American Studies and the Institute of United States Studies.

Publications in the Series

1. *Wars, Parties and Nationalism: Essays on the Politics and Society of Nineteenth-Century Latin America*
Eduardo Posada-Carbó (ed.) — 1995

2. *In Search of a New Order: Essays on the Politics and Society of Nineteenth-Century Latin America*
Eduardo Posada-Carbó (ed.) — 1998

3. *Independence and Revolution in Spanish America: Perspectives and Problems*
Anthony McFarlane and Eduardo Posada-Carbó (eds.) — 1999

4. *Law, Justice and State-Building: Judicial Institutions in Nineteenth-Century Latin America*
Eduardo Zimmermann (ed.) — 1999

5. *The Politics of Religion in an Age of Revival*
Austen Ivereigh (ed.) — 2000

6. *Rumours of Wars: Civil Conflict in Nineteenth-Century Latin America*
Rebecca Earle (ed.) — 2000

7. *The European Revolutions of 1848 and the Americas*
Guy Thomson (ed.) — 2000

8. *The Political Power of the Word: Press and Oratory in Nineteeth Century Latin America*
Iván Jaksić (ed.) — 2002

9. *Blacks and Coloureds in the Formation of National Identity in Nineteenth-Century Latin America*
Nancy Priscilla Naro (ed.) — 2002

Francisco de Miranda:
Exile and Enlightenment

edited by

John Maher

British Library Cataloguing-in-Publication Data
A catalogue record for this book is available from the British Library

ISBN 1 900039 54 0

INSTITUTE FOR THE STUDY OF THE
AMERICAS
UNIVERSITY OF LONDON · SCHOOL OF ADVANCED STUDY

Institute for the Study of the Americas
Senate House
Malet Street
London WC1E 7HU
Telephone: 020 7862 8870
Fax: 020 7862 8886
Email: americas@sas.ac.uk
Web: americas.sas.ac.uk

Contents

CONTRIBUTORS

David Bushnell, is Professor Emeritus of History at the University of Florida, and is the author of *The Making of Modern Colombia: A Nation in Spite of Itself* (Berkeley, 1993), among other books.

Malcolm Deas is a Fellow of St Antony's College, University of Oxford, and University Lecturer in the politics and government of Latin America. He has written particularly on the history of Colombia, Venezuela and Ecuador in the nineteenth and twentieth centuries.

John Lynch is Emeritus Professor of Latin American History in the University of London. He has written widely on Spanish America in the period 1750–1850. His books include *Latin America Between Colony and Nation* (London, 2001) .

John Maher is editor at the Institute for the Study of the Americas, University of London.

Edgardo Mondolfi Gudat teaches at the Universidad Metropolitana, Venezuela. He has written widely on Francisco de Miranda, most recently *Miranda en ocho contiendas* (Caracas, 2005).

Karen Racine, University of Guelph, specialises in the history and culture of the revolutionary independence period throughout Latin America and the Atlantic World. Her books include *Francisco de Miranda: A Transatlantic Life in the Age of Revolution 1750–1816* (Wilmington, DE, 2002).

Francisco de Miranda
Introduction

John Maher

Francisco de Miranda has been both neglected and overexposed. His extraordinary life in exile is the stuff of romantic fiction as he travels about North America and Europe, appearing to meet every historical figure of note — Washington, Hamilton, Adams, Thomas Paine, Jeremy Bentham, Sir Arthur Wellesley, Pitt, Potemkin, Catherine the Great, Haydn. His life, recorded in his extensive diaries and other writings, has naturally drawn many writers to his story. At the same time, however, his many ambiguities have not helped to construct a clear picture of the man. Was he self-interested adventurer or self-sacrificing idealist; dilettante or *homme sérieux*; libertine or exemplar of the Enlightenment; generalissimo or military liability? To South Americans he is both a revered Precursor of Independence and a problematic figure handed over to Spain by Bolívar to die in a Spanish dungeon. To historians and strategists his grand projects for liberating South America can too readily be portrayed as implausible and vainglorious.

As David Bushnell points out in the first chapter of this collection, Miranda has until recently been a relatively neglected figure in US historiography, and the same may be said of that in Europe. Indeed, such neglect was a central element underpinning the conference which gave rise to this collection. There have since been full-length biographies of Miranda, including a comprehensive study by one of our contributors, Karen Racine.[1] However, the concentration on individual facets of Miranda's persona in this collection provides illuminating insight into this complex character. Taken together, these contributions engage with

1 Karen Racine, *Francisco de Miranda: A Transatlantic Life in the Age of Revolution* (Wilmington, DE, 2003); Jacques de Cazotte, *Miranda 1750–1816: Histoire d'un séducteur* (Paris, 2000); Stuart F. Halpine, *The Altar of Venus: A Biography of Francisco de Miranda* (Bloomington, 2000).

the key areas of Miranda's life. Exile rendered him a traveller, with the attendant romantic aura and opportunities, though he was and conducted himself throughout primarily as a soldier and man of action, while being a cultured devotee of the Enlightenment who assembled one of the great private libraries of the time.

A brief overview of Miranda's career might suggest, as his detractors maintained at the time, a Creole amalgam of Münchausen and Casanova. His quest could be portrayed as deriving from the personal and professional frustrations that led to his joining and deserting the Spanish army, followed by the convenient embrace of both Spanish American independence and impressionable women to add romantic lustre to a self-induced and self-interested mission taking in one European court after another. This collection concentrates on specific themes in order to convey the personal qualities and aspirations of Miranda the man, and also to explore the strength of will required to persist in his distant but constant struggle for American independence without the benefits of noble birth, fortune or favourable geopolitical circumstance.

David Bushnell engages with the relationship between Francisco de Miranda and the United States — from participation with the Spanish army alongside the colonial insurgents at the battle of Pensacola in 1781, to his later escape from Spanish service via the USA in 1783–84, to his final return in 1805–06 to prepare for the abortive *Leander* expedition to Venezuela. Miranda's rather uneasy response to the mingling of the social classes which he found in the new republic reflects the rigidly stratified society of the Spanish colonies in which his family had laboured greatly to establish their social credentials. His own tendency to display airs and graces, both in person and in his role in projects for a liberated Spanish America, does seem to have been a vital ingredient in his capacity to make himself known in high places, getting his ideas heard during his years of exile. It is hard to believe that presenting himself as a humble supplicant would have had the same effect. On his second visit to the United States he became a firm friend of Alexander Hamilton and acquaintance of John Adams, and was loftily condescending about Washington.[2] Bushnell notes that Miranda's ideas for a Spanish American constitution tended to accentuate the power of the executive,

2 Racine, *Francisco de Miranda*, pp. 42–3.

the Inca. Miranda's first-hand experience of the United States was instrumental in developing his ideas about independence in Spanish America, as well as leading him to shy away from the most overtly democratic aspects of the US political system and the daily life of the country.

Miranda moved hurriedly on from North America to London. As ever, his capacity for connecting with leading figures in political and intellectual life manifested itself. John Lynch refers to a 'network of contacts' in this brief initial visit that included Jeremy Bentham, Lord Shelburne and Joseph Priestley. However, the circumstances were not propitious in 1785, and Miranda subsequently embarked on four years of European travel. On his return in 1789 he gained the ear, if not the sword, of Pitt in his attempts to involve England in a conflict with Spain that would incorporate Spanish American independence. As this failed to materialise, he went to France in 1792, not returning to England for a further six years. The Spanish alliance with France gave Miranda hope that Britain might be persuaded to involve itself in the project for Spanish American independence. That hope would wax and wane throughout the extended period of conflict between Britain and France. Miranda's connection with the British government was given concrete substance by an allowance of £500 a year. Pitt and Miranda's interests and temperaments were unlikely ever wholly to coincide, and the relationship ended in frustration for Miranda. This led to his failed expedition to Venezuela in 1806, and his dream of British involvement finally evaporated when Spain rose up against France in 1808. As a result, Miranda's friend and fellow general, the future Duke of Wellington, would head for Spain rather than South America, and Miranda himself would return to Venezuela to join Bolívar rather than with an English expeditionary force. Lynch makes clear that Miranda succeeded in making the question of Spanish America a real political and intellectual issue during his time in England. His legacy survives to this day in the shape of his London home, now Miranda House, which with its neighbouring Bolívar Hall is part of the Venezuelan Embassy in London and a beacon of Latin American cultural activity.

If Miranda had greater success in promoting his ideas than in achieving their political expression, it is worth reiterating that it is as a man of the Enlightenment that he saw and presented himself and his project. His extraordinary library was a monument to this, as was his easy familiarity with the great thinkers of his sphere. Edgardo Mondolfi Gudat also brings to the fore an aspect of Miranda's broader cultural horizons — music. He thought nothing of socialising with Jeremy Bentham and James Mill in London or giving Haydn the benefit of his views on Boccherini (before later in his travels enjoying some Boccherini quartets in the company of Potemkin). Enlightened despots may summon philosophers and composers to their presence, but for a straitened émigré to move in these circles is remarkable. It is part of that blend of self-belief and self-aggrandisement without which the ideas that he came to represent and the historic role that he played in turning South American independence from dream to reality would not have been possible. Through his cosmopolitanism Miranda conveyed to his European audience the possibilities of Spanish America, presenting himself for consideration as an ornament rather than a curiosity.

Samuel Johnson's observation that 'every man thinks meanly of himself for not having been a soldier, or not having been at sea' is mirrored by Miranda's military self-esteem. Miranda was not only a soldier in various armies; he considered himself a serious military strategist. He served with the Spanish army in Africa, North America and the Caribbean; he was made a colonel (and a count) by Catherine the Great of Russia, commanded substantial forces as a field marshal in the French revolutionary army and ended up Generalissimo of the forces of the Republic of Venezuela. He met with mixed fortunes as a military officer and commander in the field, but as Malcolm Deas points out, he was punctilious and orthodox in his military attitudes.

Such stultifying correctness was famously not reflected in Miranda's relations with women. As indicated by Karen Racine, however, he was far more than a rake or a predator. Castigated for being part Don Juan and part Don Quixote,[3] Miranda was in reality an interesting product of both his background and his time — patriarchal protector and pursuer of women on the one hand and remarkably progressive defender of the role of women in public and private life on the other. It is notable that his female friends and lovers were strong individuals. From the wealthy

3 Tomás Polanco Alcántara, *Francisco de Miranda: ¿Don Juan o Quijote?* (Caracas, 1996); José Nucete-Sardi, 'Estudio preliminar,' in Francisco de Miranda, *Textos sobre la Independencia* (Caracas, 1959), p. 22.

and independent-minded Susan Livingston in New York, by way of Catherine the Great and Lady Hester Stanhope, he could hardly be accused of preying on vulnerable women. Again, it would seem that his own self-esteem and personal enterprise took him beyond the conventions of his background and time into the territory occupied by 'transgressive lovers' rather than mere lotharios. It is surely no coincidence that both his son and his flag-ship were named Leander, after Hero's mythological lover — a romantic paragon both as swain and in his fatal determination to pursue the object of his desire in the face of physical and metaphysical obstacles, even if this could only be achieved in death.

Miranda has been both idealised and derided, carved in marble as a hero of Latin American Independence and caricatured as a self-serving and self-regarding adventurer. It would, though, be hard to deny that, if he were indeed self-interested, he signally failed to exploit his talents to achieve prosperity or comfort. He turned down Catherine the Great's offer of 10,000 roubles a year and her imperial favour; he took up arms in revolutionary France and awaited execution in the Bastille; he sailed at the head of expeditionary forces to Venezuela not once but twice, rather than rest on his hard-earned laurels as prophet of Spanish American Independence and leave the action to younger acolytes. He remains a figure of considerable fascination, too supple and significant to be shoehorned into neat shape. By focusing minutely and collectively on individual aspects of his life and work this collection aims to convey something of the breadth of Francisco de Miranda and his undertaking.

Chronology

1750	Born in Caracas, where he remains until 1771.
1771–80	Serves in the Spanish army in Spain.
1780–83	Serves with Spanish forces in the Antilles.
1783–84	First visit to the USA.
1785–92	Travels to Europe (Britain, Holland, Hungary, Italy, Turkey, Russia, Scandinavia, Prussia, Switzerland, France).
1792	Appointed field marshal in the French Revolutionary Army.

1793–95	Imprisoned in France.
1798	Leaves France for England.
1800–01	Returns to France, imprisoned and subsequently released.
1801–05	Lives in London.
1805–06	Travels to the USA to embark on the *Leander* expedition to Venezuela.
1807	Returns to Britain.
1810–12	Returns to Caracas to fight for independence from Spain.
1812–16	Spanish prisoner, dying in La Carraca prison, Cadiz, on Bastille Day 1816.

1

Francisco de Miranda and the United States: The Venezuelan Precursor and the Precursor Republic

David Bushnell

There has been a notable lack of attention paid to Francisco de Miranda by US scholars. This circumstance is perhaps curious and certainly unfair, since of all the first-rank leaders of Latin American independence none knew the United States so well, or had such important dealings in the United States, as Francisco de Miranda. Moreover, his views on the United States, as we shall see, were generally favourable. Yet he is a totally unknown figure at the level of popular culture — where, to be sure, only Simón Bolívar and Fidel Castro among Latin American political leaders enjoy some name recognition — and he is clearly not as well known as he deserves to be, even among students of Latin American history.

There is (or rather was, prior to Karen Racine's biography)[1] in that last regard one rather important exception, in the work of William Spence Robertson, whose two-volume *Life of Miranda* remains important.[2] The very breadth of Robertson's study may well have been a disincentive to other scholars who might have been tempted to work on the same topic. Some years later, Joseph Thorning contributed another Miranda biography, aimed at a more general reading public.[3] Prior to Racine's study, the only recent contribution to Miranda studies by a compatriot of mine is the work of Mario Rodríguez, '*William Burke' and*

1 Karen Racine, *Francisco de Miranda: A Transatlantic Life in the Age of Revolution* (Wilmington, DE, 2003).

2 *The Life of Miranda*, 2 vols. (Chapel Hill, NC, 1929). Hereafter cited as *Life*.

3 Joseph Thorning, *Miranda: World Citizen* (Gainesville, FL, 1952).

Francisco de Miranda: The Word and the Deed in Spanish America's Emancipation,[4] which was concerned not so much with Miranda himself as with British thinking about Spanish American independence, and the influence of that thinking on the course of the movement.

All this, to repeat, does not seem fair, but then any figure who shared the stage with Simón Bolívar, as Miranda did, is bound to be overshadowed. But I would still argue that Miranda's activities in, and ideas about, the United States are significant, and worth examining in new contexts.

The first of Miranda's activities in what would become the United States was his participation as a Spanish officer in the battle of Pensacola in May 1781, during the War of the Anglo-American Revolution. After the combined force representing the kingdom of Spain and the English colonial insurgents took the town, Miranda proceeded to buy some books there — books in English, in which he already had some competence, and all in keeping with his character as a voracious reader of encyclopaedic interests. He also purchased a few slaves in Pensacola, four to be exact, which was more than he needed for personal service and suggests that he was not yet opposed either to slavery as an institution or to the slave trade.[5]

Nevertheless, the part played by Miranda in the Pensacola campaign did not afford him any significant exposure to Anglo-American society, Pensacola being a small military outpost only recently acquired by Great Britain from Spain. Much the same can be said concerning his later participation in the Spanish seizure of the Bahamas, again in collaboration with Anglo-American revolutionaries. Indeed his relationship with the latter in the Bahamian campaign gave rise to at least one serious misunderstanding, one that resulted in a challenge to a duel from a South Carolinian officer when Miranda later turned up in Charleston. But Miranda was able to defuse the conflict with a seemingly satisfactory explanation of his conduct before the encounter could take place.[6]

Certainly for the Precursor that episode was nothing new: after all, he had already accumulated a long list of personal quarrels and antago-

4 Mario Rodríguez, '*William Burke*' *and Francisco de Miranda: The Word and Deed in Spanish America's Emancipation* (Lanham, MD, 1994).

5 *Life*, vol. I, p. 22.

6 *Ibid.*, pp. 25, 35–6.

nisms in Spanish service, which in turn hastened his decision to leave Spanish territory altogether and embark on the world travels that took him first of all to the Atlantic seaboard of the early United States. He arrived in North Carolina in June 1783 and ultimately sailed to England from Boston in December 1784. He would return to the United States once more, in 1805–06 in preparation for his ill-fated *Leander* expedition to liberate Venezuela, but his first visit was much the longest, and there can be no doubt of its critical importance in the formation of his views concerning the United States, even when this involved simply the confirmation of ideas he had already formed. Since the country had just ended its war of independence and had not yet adopted a definitive constitution, Miranda did not observe its political system in final shape, but he observed with intense interest the political practices of the various states (ex-colonies) that were loosely joined together under the Articles of Confederation, as well as salient features of social and economic life. And, though not an uncritical observer, he liked most of what he saw.

Simón Bolívar once summed up his own impressions of the United States, as formed during the visit he made to many of the same places as Miranda during 1806–07, saying that it was in the United States that for the first time he observed 'rational liberty'.[7] It may or may not be significant that Miranda, in a retrospective comment on his part, emphasised not the achievement of liberty, rational or otherwise, but the eminently successful 'pursuit of happiness', to cite another of the overriding objectives set forth in the Declaration of Independence. To be exact, he wrote to a personal correspondent that 'out of the share of happiness allotted to mankind, the people of North America enjoy the best portion perhaps of any other I know!'[8] In the same letter, written in 1789, he claimed with some exaggeration to have 'visited almost every society in Europe, Asia Minor and Egypt', so the tribute was intended to reflect a sweeping comparative perspective.

7 Letter of Chargé Beaufort T. Watts to Secretary of State, Cartagena, 10 March 1828, in William R. Manning (ed.), *Diplomatic Correspondence of the United States Concerning the Independence of the Latin American Nations*, 3 vols. (New York, 1925), vol. II, p. 1322.

8 Cited in Francisco de Miranda, *The Diary of Francisco de Miranda: Tour of the United States 1783–1784* (New York, 1928), p. 169, n. 651. Hereafter cited as *Diary*.

At the time of that first visit, Miranda still had not travelled so widely, but he had been to Spain, to a string of Spanish outposts in North Africa, to British-occupied Gibraltar, and in the New World, in addition to his native Venezuela, to Cuba and Florida, Jamaica and the Bahamas. He had also read widely and had obtained additional prior impressions of the early United States through personal encounters with its citizens and by conversation with other observers. Not least, he already had a better command of the English language than Bolívar had when he carried out his own North American journey.

In the diary of his trip, Miranda attributed the high degree of happiness enjoyed by North Americans in part to their political institutions (on which more below) but also quite notably to the relative degree of social and economic equality that prevailed among them. Although he was not a bona fide egalitarian, as will be seen, he did see a connection between a more equitable land distribution and material prosperity. This emerges most clearly in his discussion of New Jersey, where he actually did not spend much time, using it principally, as people still do today, as a land bridge between Pennsylvania and New York. Neither then nor later has New Jersey had for most people any clear-cut image, either positive or negative. But it did for Miranda, who contrasted the 'indifferent' quality of its soil with the comfort, industry and robust good health of the inhabitants, and as the principal explanation for this happy state of affairs pointed out that the land was divided 'in general into small portions which they call farms, from which it results that the land is much better cultivated, and the number of houses is much more, though not of sumptuous appearance as in other countries (Havana and South Carolina, let us suppose)'.[9] By the reference to South Carolina, he gave recognition that within North America itself happiness was not evenly divided from place to place, yet he returned to discuss the advantages of relative economic equality when he got to New England, where the benefits of widespread property ownership offset not only the poor soil — actually a good bit poorer than in New Jersey — but also the cold climate, which Miranda, who had not yet spent a winter in Denmark, found very hard to bear.[10] Also in New England, Miranda

9 *Diary*, pp. 49–50

10 *Ibid.*, pp. 110, 129, 131.

noted with approval such signs of widespread popular education as the prevalence of public libraries even in small towns. In one of these he remarked that the books of its library were certainly more often read than those of the Escorial library in Spain.[11]

Despite the disparaging reference that he made to Havana as compared to New Jersey, Miranda's experiences in the United States do not seem to have made him an agrarian reformer in his subsequent proposals for Spanish America. It is also worth noting that his travels through the United States never suggested any general considerations on the subject of slavery, and neither did he comment on the legal rights and disabilities of free non-white inhabitants. However, he did point out two cases that in his view demonstrated the intrinsic capacity of all human beings, regardless of race, when he underscored the outstanding service of Native Americans on New England whaling crews and the literary accomplishment of a Boston poetess who happened to be black.[12]

It was hardly because of these examples that he later called for the granting of legal equality to Indians and free *pardos* in Spanish America, but such comments during the North American trip do at least foreshadow his later position.

It needs to be added here that Miranda's theoretical appreciation of human equality did not save him from feeling personally uncomfortable at times with its manifestations. There could, in effect, be too much of a good thing. Thus, in one of his earliest observations after reaching the United States, he noted with disapproval how in a North Carolina militia exercise the local gentry mixed freely with the filthiest and lowest class of people, even drinking from the very same glass. It was 'impossible', he said, 'to conceive without seeing it a more purely democratic assembly'.[13] He generally managed to avoid drinking with inferiors himself, but he did have a close call when the Boston stage that he was taking halted for a meal stop, and in a seemingly excessive 'spirit of republicanism' all the passengers and even the mule driver himself sat down to eat at the same table of the roadside inn. Miranda explained that he had to make special arrangement in order for his own servant to eat separately.[14]

11 *Ibid.*, p. 86.

12 *Ibid.*, pp. 96, 119.

13 *Ibid.*, p. 6.

14 *Ibid.*, pp. 82–3.

Another way in which Miranda believed that North Americans sometimes carried the spirit of equality too far was their disinclination to give due recognition to superior merit. He gives more than one example of this, but my favourite, naturally, is the one referring to my own illustrious forebear, David Bushnell — or 'Bushenall', Miranda calls him — who had devised a primitive version of the submarine to serve in our own struggle for independence. The 'Turtle', as Bushnell/Bushenall called it, failed to sink the British battleship that it went against, but this was no reason in the Venezuelan's opinion (or in mine) for not awarding its inventor some sort of special prize or honour. Miranda's final comment on the matter was a sardonic '¡Viva la democracia!'[15] Yet if the tendency to undervalue outstanding merit was a general national characteristic, Miranda also saw a conspicuous exception in the adulation lavished upon the Father of His Country, George Washington himself. Miranda was able to meet Washington and admired him, but he still considered the reserved and overly circumspect general to be an overrated hero.[16]

Miranda likewise saw a relative lack of talent among judges in Rhode Island, whom he considered clearly inferior in calibre to the lawyers who argued cases before them: this he blamed on their low pay, which would be another instance of inadequate recognition of merit.[17] But the failure to recognise achievement was obviously not just a social and cultural phenomenon but also a political problem, and in this connection Miranda had some rather pungent observations on the deficit of merit among those holding elective office in the North American republic. One of the worst examples was the New Hampshire state assembly which he visited at a time when the people's chosen representatives were standing in deepest respect to hear a memorial presented by eight vain and ignorant Protestant ecclesiastics, thereby revealing their own severe lack of enlightenment.[18] Yet even more interesting was the discussion he had with the Boston brewer and revolutionary agitator Sam Adams, who had to agree with him that while in principle the basis of a democracy was virtue, in practice in his country 'no place whatever is indicat-

15 *Ibid.*, p. 90. For another example, p. 131.

16 *Ibid.*, p. 109.

17 *Ibid.*, pp. 39–40. Lafayette, it also seemed to Miranda, was a 'mediocre' figure about whom 'simple people' made far too great a fuss (p. 121).

18 *Ibid.*, p. 109.

ed for the latter, and on the contrary all dignities and power were given to property, which is just the poison of such a Republic!'[19] This did not mean that government was entirely in the hands of a commercial oligarchy, for elsewhere Miranda noted that the Massachusetts legislature had been made up of such people as a tailor, an innkeeper and a blacksmith. The fact was simply that while in most states the right to vote and hold office was initially limited to property owners, property was widely enough distributed that this requirement was not incompatible with what for the period was a high degree of political democracy; the problem was instead that property was more widely distributed than wisdom.[20] At least it was not wholly concentrated in the hands of the very wealthy, concerning whom Miranda had harsh words, accusing them of an irresponsible addiction to imported luxuries that endangered the new nation's balance of payments.[21]

On returning to the United States in 1805, Miranda again expressed concern over the conduct of the upper economic strata and went so far as to suggest in conversation with the Philadelphia medical doctor and political figure Benjamin Rush that a 'plutocracy' was emerging at the expense of that 'simplicity of customs' which he had admired on his earlier visit.[22] Nevertheless, Miranda's original assessment of the political system of the United States had been definitely more positive than negative, despite whatever problems and shortcomings he noted, and those first impressions (never entirely dispelled) certainly left their mark in the formation of his political thought. In this regard he repeatedly cited the benefit of free institutions as something enjoyed by all the new land and powerfully contributing to its people's happiness, albeit for the most part he did so generically rather than spelling out precisely what the freedom consisted of. He further took it for granted that this priceless gift was a mark of the former 13 colonies' British heritage. Quite typically, he lauded the courts of South Carolina for adhering to the 'admirable system of the British constitution'.[23] And where he criticised

19 *Ibid.* p. 118.

20 *Ibid.*, pp. 120–1.

21 *Ibid.*, pp. 117–18.

22 Manuel Pérez Vila, 'Miranda en Filadelfia,' *Boletín de la Academia Nacional de Historia de Venezuela*, vol. 42, no. 167 (July–September 1959), pp. 363–4.

23 *Diary*, pp. 22–3.

the excessive democracy of the institutions that he was observing, it was for their departure from the 'admirable balance of the British constitution', which to Miranda was apparently not just a balance of governmental powers but a balance of social forces.[24]

The two specific dimensions of freedom that are singled out for praise most often in Miranda's North American diary are religious toleration and (of obvious importance to an inveterate traveller) the unrestricted freedom of movement. The prevailing religious liberty he inevitably contrasted with the sorry condition of the Spanish empire lying in the grip of the Inquisition. He approvingly noted, for example, how a proto-Unitarian preacher in Boston whom he did not personally consider very intelligent could voice a string of absurdities and yet people were merely amused by him — whereas in Spain's dominions he would have been burned at the stake. Miranda deplored (and again Sam Adams had deplored with him) the logical contradiction between the freedom of worship and of religious opinion that existed everywhere and the all-too-common religious tests for holding office.[25] He likewise repeatedly deplored the numerous restrictions on Sabbath-day activities that he kept encountering and that were to him a sign of the persistence of superstition even in this generally enlightened land, and he once declared himself simply fed up ('harto y fatigado de Yglesia hasta los ojos'[26]) with the constant church-going imposed on him by Anglo-American customs. Yet even with these limitations religious liberty made an inestimable contribution to the high degree of happiness that he discerned as he travelled. And as for the ease of travel, Miranda commented again and again on the fact that he, a foreigner, could go from place to place, by ship or on land, without facing police commissars or customs inspectors or any other of the impediments that travellers would face in the kingdoms of Europe, to say nothing of Spanish America.[27]

24 *Ibid.*, p. 25. Though he never abandoned his admiration for British institutions, Miranda did observe — in his discussions with Benjamin Rush already referred to — that on the basis of living in England he had come to realise that the idealised version of the British constitution found in the writing of Montesquieu bore little relation to reality. See Pérez Vila, 'Miranda en Filadelfia,' p. 365.

25 *Diary*, p. 118 (and on New Hampshire, p. 134).

26 *Ibid.*, p. 81.

27 *Ibid.*, pp. 14, 58.

Both because he tended to regard the positive features of the United States political system as essentially by-products of the British heritage and because he believed that the new republic sometimes took social equality and political democracy too far, the institutions that Miranda himself ultimately proposed for Spanish America owed little explicitly to the United States model. The first of his projects was put before the British authorities in 1790, after the US constitutional convention had completed its handiwork and having in common with the latter mainly the fact that it assumed a written frame of government rather than an unwritten constitution like the British that he among others so much admired. There was also some similarity in the amendment procedures that he outlined, which were a necessary corollary of the mere fact that the constitution was to be written and thus without strict parallel in the British system. But for the rest Miranda proposed not a republic but a constitutional monarchy headed by a descendant of the Incas, with a senate that was not strictly hereditary but still roughly comparable to the House of Lords in that the members were to be named for life by the emperor (that is, the 'Inca') himself. An accompanying proclamation drafted probably (according to Robertson) by Miranda's English collaborator Thomas Pownall, but no doubt approved by Miranda in all essentials, included provisions for the temporary organisation of liberated territory under governors who would be assisted by councils chosen through indirect election. The proclamation further promised abolition of the Inquisition, state monopolies and Indian tribute, all of which would have been in line with North American practice although certainly not suggested only by it.[28]

Miranda presented a second, more detailed draft proposal for the government of liberated territories to the British official Nicholas Vansittart in 1801, ostensibly on behalf of a Spanish American revolutionary council. In response to an initial inquiry by Vansittart as to his long-term political objectives, Miranda had observed that 'a system of government similar to that of the United States would be very popular and perhaps the most convenient'.[29] And the scheme that he then sub-

28 *Life*, vol. I, pp. 103–05. This project was not preserved in Miranda's personal archive but in the Chatham Manuscripts of the National Archives in London.

29 *Life*, vol. I, p. 223.

mitted was indeed a bit closer to the US model than the earlier plan had been, even if far from an exact copy. It envisaged a 'provisional government' featuring regional assemblies to be elected, again indirectly, by all citizens, specifically including free blacks (provided they had been born of free parents) and Indians, who had an annual income equivalent to at least the modest sum of 36 pesos; and also local-level or municipal corporations much like the colonial *cabildos* but augmented with additional members representing the Indians and collared *castas*. These arrangements would ultimately be complemented by a definitive 'federal' government, designed for an independent American 'Empire'. In this the suffrage would be limited to property-owners, and the central legislative branch, designated 'Imperial Diet', consisted of a single chamber whose members were chosen by the provincial assemblies. The central executive power was to be headed not by one but by two 'Incas.' The position was no longer hereditary, however, any more than were the national legislators; instead the 'Incas' were chosen by the latter for five-year terms. This dual executive was clearly modelled after the consuls of the ancient Roman republic, and the presence of 'censors', 'ediles' and 'quaestors' among the other officials of the federation was further evidence of classical inspiration.[30]

The fact that Miranda termed the overall government 'federal' reflected the influence, perhaps, of North American terminology. But this was hardly a federation in the sense of the US constitution, with its explicit division of powers between the central authorities and the various states, although it may be that some partial autonomy was envisaged for regional or provincial governments — the proposal just did not deal concretely with the relationship between the centre and the regions. For the rest, in the constitution itself and in another accompanying proclamation, Miranda reiterated the basic reforms put forward in 1790 — abolition of tribute and Inquisition, equality of the races before the law — and even included a few more, such as the introduction of trial by jury. He also added one new feature in the form of a provision for naming a 'dictator' to take charge in the event of grave national

30 Francisco de Miranda, *Textos sobre la independencia* (Caracas, 1959; Biblioteca, 13), pp. 67–77. There had also been mention of 'quaestors' and so forth in the 1790 plan.

emergency. Curiously enough, according to a marginal note on the copy of the proposal in Miranda's papers, the dictatorial provision was suggested by two of his United States confidants and correspondents, Henry Knox and Alexander Hamilton. Even so, it was not taken from any US constitutional precedent, which did not exist; the model once again was obviously the ancient Roman republic, whose institutions were as familiar to the North Americans as to Miranda himself.[31]

Finally, Miranda once again included a procedure for constitutional amendments. This was still the only feature of strictly North American provenance, although the elimination of hereditary and life-term officials brought the plan closer to the United States (or for that matter the French Revolutionary) model than to that of the British constitutional monarchy. In any case, Miranda presented this same project, Incas and all, to the first Venezuelan congress, after the independence movement finally got under way and he had returned one more time to his homeland. He was even made a member of the congressional committee that was to draft a new frame of government, but the other members do not seem to have taken his ideas seriously. Nor did Miranda take a significant part in the debates leading up to the formal adoption of Venezuela's Constitution of 1811, no doubt in part because he realised that the congress would not be receptive to what he had to say. In the end he merely submitted a brief written statement indicating his displeasure with the finished constitution on the grounds that in it the powers of government were not properly balanced and were not suited to Venezuela.[32]

By his protest Miranda obviously meant, at a minimum, that the executive was too weak. This was one feature in which the Venezuelan constitution departed notably from the North American model, in that it placed supreme power in the hands of a triumvirate rather than a single president. Its federal structure, on the other hand, did bear an obvious superficial resemblance to the US constitution, but clearly was not the type of federation Miranda had in mind when drafting his own project of a 'federal' empire for Spanish America. Indeed, at the level of an ex-captaincy-general such as Venezuela, Miranda was undoubtedly a

31 *Life*, vol. I, pp. 224–30.

32 Caracciolo Parra Pérez, *Historia de la Primera República de Venezuela*, vol. II (Caracas, 1959; Biblioteca, 20), pp. 120–1, 176–7, 185–6.

centralist like Bolívar, particularly in the very midst of a struggle for existence. At least he would finally receive in his own hands the dictatorial emergency power that he recommended in his earlier proposal and that he attributed to the suggestion of US acquaintances though not the example of the US constitution.

A final facet of Miranda's attitude towards the United States was the belief that he shared with virtually all the leaders of Latin American independence to the effect that the prior independence of the 13 English colonies demonstrated the desirability and feasibility of their doing the same. Like many others, he was fond of repeating the cliché that if a mere three million English colonists (conveniently overlooking their French and Spanish allies of whom he had himself been one) were able to vanquish a major European power, then it would be all the more easy for 15 million Spanish Americans to break loose from a decadent mother country whose population was inferior to theirs.[33] He likewise assumed, as did most of the others, that the people and government of the United States — 'our neighbours, our brothers in liberty, and, in fine, our own compatriots' — could only rejoice if Spanish America followed their example and would in fact lend help to the enterprise.[34]

Miranda later wrote that his project for Spanish American independence took shape precisely during his original visit to the United States.[35] He does not say this in so many words in his travel diary, but his increasing alienation from Spain does come through in the observations he recorded while in the United States, and in the course of his meetings with a remarkable number of men who had taken active roles in US independence it is scarcely conceivable that the possibility of Spanish America following that example would not have repeatedly come up — at Miranda's initiative or theirs. Moreover, he seems to have discussed quite concrete details, including details of potential North American cooperation, with such men as Knox and Hamilton; and he claimed to have received encouragement from them.[36] No doubt they did encour-

33 For example, *Textos sobre la independencia*, p. 125.

34 *Life*, vol. I, p. 165.

35 *Textos sobre la independencia*, p. 46.

36 *Life*, vol. I, pp. 53–5, pp. 126–7; Tomás Polanco Alcántara, *Francisco de Miranda: bosquejo de una biografía ¿Don Juan o Don Quijote?* (Caracas, 1996), pp. 260–2.

age him, though not necessarily with firm commitments, as can be inferred from a marginal note jotted by Hamilton on one of Miranda's letters. In it this North American sympathiser recalled that he had 'frequent conversation' with the Venezuelan on the subject of Spanish American liberation, but added simply, 'I presume [that I] expressed ideas favourable to the object and perhaps gave an opinion that it was one to which the United States would look with interest…'[37]

Miranda, on his part, did not anticipate a massive intervention by the United States on Spanish America's behalf: more than once he suggested that what he looked for was something like the informal assistance rendered by France to the English American revolutionists prior to France's official entry into the struggle.[38] He in any case remained in touch with a number of influential North Americans, by correspondence or in personal meetings, all the time that he was in London or on the continent of Europe; and though his primary objective throughout was to obtain the collaboration of Great Britain for his grand design, he never abandoned his hope that the former British colonies would likewise play a role. He was delighted whenever a crisis loomed in relations between the United States and Spain, and would then refurbish his hopes for North American assistance until the crisis subsided. And it was the coincidence between one such crisis, over maritime and border disputes, and a new bout of discouragement concerning the prospect of concrete assistance from the British government that caused Miranda in 1805 to abandon his base of agitation and intrigue in London and make another visit to the United States.[39]

After his arrival in New York, Miranda lost no time in renewing contacts and in making arrangements to recruit personnel and acquire necessary equipment for an expedition to revolutionise Venezuela. He recognised that he would need at least the tacit forbearance of the government itself — for it to 'wink at' his activities, as he kept saying, as if he relished displaying his command of that particular idiomatic expression. He managed to see both President Jefferson and his secretary of state, James Madison, and he did not hesitate to report that they indeed

37 Cited in *Life*, vol. I, p. 177.

38 For example, *Life*, vol. I, p. 295.

39 *Life*, vol. I, 160–87, 293 and *passim*.

were prepared to 'wink'. Yet in their own accounts of the meetings with Miranda they claimed to have made clear that while they could not help but sympathise with Miranda's objective, and private citizens were free to provide any help not forbidden by law, they could not countenance any outright violation of the law. Thus Miranda was able to contract for supplies and recruit followers, but after the *Leander* sailed, two of his backers — one a federal official — were indicted and brought to trial for transgressing the country's neutrality legislation. Their guilt was obvious enough. Both were duly acquitted.[40]

Though Miranda's expedition sailed from the United States and was initially outfitted by his US backers, before he at length admitted failure and returned to London he really obtained more help from British than US sources — thanks to British officials in the West Indies who simply assumed, without explicit instructions, that they were acting in accordance with the unstated policy of the British government. Even so, Miranda certainly did not give up his hope for US assistance of one sort or another, and in 1812, when he was serving as head of Venezuela's First Republic, one object of his diplomacy was to make this hope a reality.[41] Moreover, the United States actually went so far as to send official, and not simply informal, help to the struggling independent nation. But instead of arms or troops or other military assistance against Spain, it was humanitarian relief voted by the Congress in Washington after the disastrous Holy Thursday earthquake. Unfortunately, the shipments arrived just as the First Republic was collapsing, so that the supplies, mostly US flour, ended up in the hands of the restored Spanish regime.[42]

Before the independence struggle was brought to a successful conclusion by Miranda's successors, the United States had provided other assistance, mainly in the form of military supplies (sold not donated) and the volunteer services of seamen who took up privateering duty (for their own as well as Venezuela's profit). One can only conclude

40 *Life*, vol. I, pp. 293–301; Polanco Alcántara, *Francisco de Miranda*, pp. 461–7; Archivo del General Miranda, 24 vols. (Caracas, 1929–50), vol. XVII, pp. 284–92.

41 Parra Pérez, *Historia de la Primera República*, vol. II, pp. 407–9.

42 Harold A. Bierck, Jr., 'The First Instance of US Foreign Aid: Venezuelan Relief in 1812,' *Inter-American Economic Affairs.*, vol. IX, no. 1 (Summer 1955), pp. 47–59.

therefore that Miranda had been overly optimistic about the possible scope of US collaboration, even if not mistaken in his assessment of general US sympathy for the Spanish American cause. In all this, of course, he anticipated — was the Precursor of — the thinking of other independence leaders. He was likewise a Precursor of those, like Bolívar, who did not consider US institutions readily transferable to Spanish America, although he did not develop his thoughts on this matter as fully as Bolívar did: he simply did not borrow widely from the United States in his own political proposals. And if he failed to do so, it was in considerable part because he knew the United States better than almost any of his Latin American contemporaries, and accordingly appreciated the underlying differences between the two societies.

2

Francisco de Miranda: The London Years

John Lynch

Miranda's World

The public life of Francisco de Miranda defies a single narrative line. Long before historians learned this, his contemporaries knew it. How were they to deal with him? As a soldier, a politician, an intellectual, an activist, an anglophile, a revolutionary, an exile in waiting or a dedicated traveller? In these multiple roles he was unpredictable and impulsive; his voluminous documentation and archive are a challenge as well as an inducement to research, and his decisions call for careful analysis. All this applies to his London years, which at first glance are a confusing mixture of events, ideas and emotions.

The historian looking for order and meaning has a guide in one of Miranda's own works, at once a source and an apologia: *South American Emancipation*, published in London in 1810. The editor was José María Antepara, an émigré from Guayaquil, but as in other such publications the real author was Miranda, who supplied the material and the ideas and who for tactical reasons hid his identity behind the names of others. The book consists of documents, from Miranda's own collection, recording his contribution to South American independence: 'he has dedicated to this one design almost the whole of his life and has been the prime mover in every scheme that has been proposed for the emancipation of the Spanish colonies in America'.[1] Now it was important to refute falsehoods spread by his enemies and to present a favourable

1 José María Antepara, *South American Emancipation. Documents Historical and Explanatory, Shewing the Designs which have been in Progress and the Exertions made by General Miranda, for the Attainment of that Object during the Last Twenty-Five Years* (London, 1810), p. 14.

account of his activities at a time when the Spanish authorities were pressing their British allies to expel him as a subversive. The compilation is divided into various themes, including (1) Miranda's experiences in France, emphasising his liberal anti-Jacobin role; (2) his relations with politicians of the United States; (3) the projects presented by him to the British government; (4) the expedition to Venezuela; (5) contacts with other Spanish Americans in London and efforts to promote his ideas. Three of these themes are developed in the present chapter: Miranda's projects for the liberation of South America on which he lobbied the British government; his political ideas and their presentation; and his role as a focal point of Spanish American interests in London. Finally, the question of how London reacted to Miranda will be considered.

Plans and Prospects

Miranda's first relations with Britain were fed on hope rather than promise. As a Venezuelan creole his disillusion with Spain was personal and ideological. At the same time as he abandoned his career in the Spanish army, the victim of manifest injustice, so he began to question the legitimacy of Spanish rule in America, now starkly contrasted with the newly won freedom which he saw in the United States. Here, in New York in 1784, he conceived a plan 'for the independence and liberty of the whole Spanish American continent, with the cooperation of England', a country which he did not yet know except as an enemy in the recent war, but which for his new purposes possessed naval power and political appeal. With this in mind he left the United States and arrived in London on 1 February 1785. He soon found that the time was not right for a formal approach. As he later explained, 'The embarrassment and disgust that prevailed in the nation because of the loss of its colonies and the heavy expenses of the recent war did not provide an opportunity for the promotion of a project of such magnitude. So while I waited I resolved to occupy my time by carefully examining the various governments and political systems of Europe.'[2]

2 Miranda, 'Datos a Gennsoné para un Manifiesto sobre la Independencia hispano-americana,' Paris, 10 October 1792, *Archivo del General Miranda* (24 vols., Caracas, Havana, 1929–50), vol. VIII, pp. 8–11.

Miranda's six months in England were not wasted. He began to assemble a network of contacts: politicians, army officers, journalists, reformers, including Jeremy Bentham, Lord Shelburne, Joseph Priestley and John Turnbull, a wealthy merchant whom he had met in Spain and would prove to be a friend in need. He wrote of these months, 'Philosophy, government, academies of science, sessions of parliament and the company of scholars and statesmen occupy all my time at present with much profit, and to some extent they help to mitigate the pain of harsh adversity.'[3] An anonymous article placed in the *Political Herald and Review* promoted his cause and his image. It referred to the presence in London of 'a Spanish American of great consequence and possessed of the confidence of his fellow citizens who aspires to the glory of being the deliverer of his country. He is a man of sublime views and penetrating understanding, skilled in the ancient and modern languages, conversant in books and acquainted with the world.'[4]

Miranda spent the years 1785–89 travelling in Europe, reading, observing, learning and establishing his reputation as a man of the Enlightenment. His Diary for this time is a graphic guide to pre-revolutionary Europe. He returned to London in June 1789 and took advantage of the good offices of Thomas Pownall, ex-governor of Massachusetts, authority on imperial affairs and author of a work sympathetic to the independence of Spanish America, to make contact with the political establishment. It was a good moment. The Nootka Sound dispute brought Britain to the verge of war with Spain over rival claims to colonial territory and the British government was ready to consider the possibility of attacking Spain in the Americas. Miranda had two meetings with the prime minister, William Pitt, on 14 February and 6 May, but there was no meeting of minds. Miranda was attempting to mobilise a liberating expedition which would replace Spanish rule by a single constitutional monarchy headed by a hereditary 'Inca' emperor

3 Miranda to Arrieta, 20 June 1785, *Colombeia*, ed. Josefina Rodríguez de Alonso (Caracas, 1978–), vol. III, p. 399.

4 Reproduced in Mario Rodríguez, '*William Burke' and Francisco de Miranda: The Word and the Deed in Spanish America's Emancipation* (Lanham, 1994), p. 11, who attributes it to Colonel William Stephens Smith, secretary of the United States legation in London, friend and travelling companion of Miranda.

with a bicameral congress. He projected a special alliance with Britain 'to shake off the infamous oppression in which Spain keeps South America, denying office, movement, and freedom of thought'. Britain would supply 12–15,000 infantry and 15 frigates in return for financial and commercial concessions from the new state. He recommended Spanish American Jesuits, in resentful exile in Italy, as liaison agents between the English and the creoles.

Pitt listened and learned. He was seeking a possible theatre of war against Spain and a means of challenging its claims to monopoly of trade and territory on the west coast of North America; and he saw Miranda as a source of information and leverage against Spain. Ultimate objectives — conquest or emancipation — were unclear. They remained unclear, for the two powers reached agreement in October 1790 when Spain abandoned exclusive claims to the west coast of North America in return for a British undertaking to prevent illicit trade with the Spanish colonies. Miranda was left frustrated and fuming. In 1791 he summarised his hopes in a letter to Pitt: 'My views are now, and always were, to promote the happiness and liberty of my own Country (South-America), excessively oppressed; and in so doing to offer also great commercial advantages to Great Britain.'[5] The government was unmoved. 'Pitt is a monster', he complained, 'I am sold by a treaty of commerce with Spain.'[6] He failed to obtain a government pension and in March 1792 he left for France.

In January 1798 Miranda returned to the fold from a now hostile France and was warmly received by Pitt. The international situation seemed to have turned in his favour again: since 1796 when Spain joined France in a satellite role in war against Britain, the Spanish empire openly entered British calculations as a possible theatre of war where a diversionary blow might be struck against French power. It was now that Henry Dundas, secretary of war, emerged as one of the leading advocates of a Spanish American policy, seconded by Nicholas Vansittart, a prominent young lawyer and member of parliament, and Thomas

5 Miranda to Pitt, 26 August 1791, 17 March 1792, *Archivo Miranda*, vol. XV, pp. 132–7, 142–4, detailing his grievances.

6 William Spence Robertson, *The Life of Miranda*, 2 vols. (Chapel Hill, NC, 1929), vol. I, p. 112.

Picton, the first British governor of Trinidad, who was convinced that 'a great moral revolution, the forerunner of a political one, has already taken place in that country [Venezuela]'.[7]

Miranda reached London on 15 January and was received by Pitt at his country seat on the following day. He now proposed an even more ambitious project: the invasion of Spanish America by Britain and the United States, to be joined by Spanish American forces fighting for liberation and independence. Miranda wanted 27 British ships and an expeditionary force of 12,000 British troops and 5,000 North American; the latter would focus on the isthmus of Panama, while the British would mount a pincer movement from Venezuela and Chile.[8] Central America and Mexico would welcome their liberators in one big final assault. And the result? South Americans would form an immediate nation and reward their British liberators with a sum of £30 million sterling. Both Britain and the USA would obtain favourable trading terms.

The triple alliance never materialised. Rufus King, the United States minister in London, was vaguely interested but his government disliked the idea of collaborating with Britain. The British government was noncommittal. Pitt's reservations were understandable. In that vast theatre of operations, whom did Miranda represent? Who could take seriously his claim to be the agent of a revolutionary junta, composed of 'deputies' from Spanish America, which was supposed to have met in Paris in December 1797? Pitt was also concerned less with emancipation, for which there is little evidence that he entertained any serious sympathy, as it would mean the introduction of 'the French system' into Spanish America. To reassure him Miranda stated that the form of government of a liberated Spanish America would be 'very similar to that of Great Britain'.[9] His military proposals were equally unrealistic. Pitt showed no more than polite interest. The essential issue in the eyes of the British government was the danger of French revolutionary influence. It was no part of its policy to evoke the spirit of the French Revolution in Spanish America at the very time it was fighting it in

7 Picton to General Prigge, 22 April 1799, British Library (BL), Add. 36870, ff. 20–1.

8 Plan Militar, London, August 1798, *Archivo Miranda*, vol. XV, pp. 287–95.

9 Robertson, *Life of Miranda*, vol. I, p. 169.

Europe. As long as Spain was able to preserve its empire from French penetration then Britain would not intervene in Spanish America. Miranda, frustrated in his projected triple alliance, was refused a passport to proceed to Trinidad which he saw as a base for revolutionising South America; fobbed off with a small stipend, he returned to France in November 1800, to find that he had exhausted his political capital and he was quickly expelled.

In the course of 1800–01, however, renewed fear of French intentions in the New World brought the idea of British action in Spanish America out of cold storage. The Spanish American lobby in England, a small group of interested politicians, businessmen, and naval and military personnel, was increasing its pressure. The focus of the lobby was Henry Dundas, who from 1800 argued the case for a South American expedition and, with his junior ally William Huskisson, gave the lobby an entrance to the administration. Pitt's government fell in March 1801 and was succeeded by the Addington ministry, in which the lobbyists had a distinguished advocate in Nicholas Vansittart, joint secretary of the treasury and a new friend for Miranda, who now received a yearly allowance of £500 from the government.[10] With this network Miranda was in his element; here he was among English friends and sympathisers, people who relied on him for information and could give him access to political decisions. Or so it seemed. Now, in collaboration with Thomas Pownall, he prepared a scheme of provisional government for Spanish America, a military regulation and a proclamation 'A los pueblos del continente Colombiano alias Hispanoamérica'.[11]

The proclamation exhorted Spanish Americans: 'At the present time are you not excluded from the principal public offices? Are you not subject to the insatiable rapacity of those who devour your money in order to enrich greedy foreigners at the expense of the natives of the country? Who among you have not groaned under the oppressive rule of the Gálvez, the Areches, the Piñeres, the Avalos and the Brancifortes?'[12] Miranda's scheme of government for 'Colombia' now consisted of two Incas, 'a venerable name in our country', serving for five-year terms,

10 *Ibid.*, vol. I, pp. 246–7.

11 For these three items see *Archivo Miranda*, vol. XVI, pp. 104–59.

12 *Ibid.*, vol. XVI, pp. 116–17.

one residing in the capital, the other a travelling executive. In the event of emergency or crisis the two Incas would appoint a Roman-type 'Dictator' as a troubleshooter for a year.

Meanwhile important issues of principle and policy had been building up between Miranda and the British government. First, who was to be in charge of any expedition? Miranda or a British commander? The government of Pitt or of any other prime minister would never allow a British expedition to be commanded by a foreigner. Yet Miranda could not accept a secondary position in a national project. Second, the British tended to think of Spanish America as an opportunity for conquest, Miranda for liberation. This was a fundamental contradiction which had never been resolved. Third, as the years passed Miranda became increasingly convinced that the British government simply wanted him to stand by, to pose a threat, to be kept as a deterrent to Spain rather than an ally against Spain. He saw himself as a victim of broken promises, constantly palmed off with what he called 'the mysterious pretexts of negotiations' and other diplomatic excuses, and always with the explanation that 'to revolutionise South America at this particular time would upset our policies in Europe'.[13]

The gloom of these years was suddenly pierced by the light of a new star, Sir Home Popham, a naval officer with interests in wider strategies than those espoused by the admiralty, and soon to emerge as the *enfant terrible* of the Spanish American lobby. In the course of 1803 Vansittart introduced Popham and Miranda, and the former indicated that he wished to serve 'in whatsoever expedition may be formed to establish the independence of South America'.[14] Thus began an association which invigorated Miranda's campaign and promised to bring it closer to its objectives. Popham's commitment to independence, of course, was always ambiguous; colonial conquest was more his style. This can be inferred from the plan which he submitted to the government in November 1803, when he pleaded for an expedition against

13 Miranda, *Diary*, 16 July, 5 August 1805, *ibid.*, vol. XVII, pp. 246–7, 248.

14 'Esta nota me dio Sir Home Popham este dia manifestandome su deseo de servir con migo en qualesquiera Expedición que se forme para establecer la Indp[a] de la America Meridional.' Miranda, 1 August 1803, *Archivo Miranda*, vol., XVI, pp. 325–6.

Buenos Aires in order to establish a military base ancillary to Miranda's main target, Venezuela.

Popham claimed to have 'been long in the habit of strict and confidential intimacy' with Miranda, whose projects, he believed, were marked by strong common sense.[15] He secured a private conference with Pitt and Dundas, now Viscount Melville, 'explaining all General Miranda's views', and he was instructed to consult with the Venezuelan and submit a specific scheme. This was the origin of Popham's memorandum of 14 October 1804.[16] In addition to the commercial argument for British intervention, Popham urged the strategic importance of anticipating Napoleon in Spanish America and depriving France of an important source of revenue. He referred certainly to Miranda's 'great object', the emancipation of South America, but he also urged that key positions in the subcontinent should be taken and that in addition to the major expedition to Venezuela, a subsidiary one should be sent to the Río de la Plata. These views masked a basic difference of objectives between Popham and Miranda. Miranda's suspicions were aroused by Popham's proposal to take La Guaira for Britain, 'a strange idea' which Melville also repudiated. Miranda subsequently claimed that conquest in the Río de la Plata 'may have been the plans of General Beresford and Sir Home Popham but they certainly never were those of the British Ministers I have just mentioned [Melville, Pitt and Addington], nor of mine!'[17] In any case the plan of 1804 was kept in cold storage. Even when Spain declared war on Britain (12 December 1804) and the Third Coalition was broken by Napoleon's great victories, Pitt still held back. And his indecision can only be explained by those traditional factors inhibiting British policy in Spanish America: fear of the political consequences of disrupting the area, reluctance to undertake the heavy military commitment involved and lack of conviction in the commercial argument.[18]

15 Popham, Memo, 26 November 1803, The National Archives, Kew, Chatham Papers, GD 8/345.

16 Printed in 'Miranda and the British Admiralty, 1804–1806,' *American Historical Review*, vol. 6 (1901), pp. 509–17; copy in *Archivo Miranda*, vol. XVII, pp. 85–96; Roberston, *Life of Miranda*, vol. I, p. 277.

17 Miranda to Alex. Cochrane, 4 June 1807, National Library of Scotland (NLS), Cochrane Papers 2320, f. 114.

18 John Lynch, 'British Policy and Spanish America, 1783–1808,' *Journal of Latin American Studies*, vol. 1, no. 1 (1969), pp. 1–30.

Miranda and Popham, in their separate ways, took matters into their own hands. Despairing of obtaining a decision from the British government, Miranda left England in September 1805 and in the following year, from the United States, led an abortive expedition to the coast of Venezuela. He received supply facilities and some naval support from local British authorities in the West Indies, though not enough to compensate for his failure to raise the creole population. The bishop of Mérida voiced the prejudices of the Venezuelan elite when he denounced Miranda as 'traitor to his sovereign and his country', an atheist who would appoint 'protestants and Jews' to public office.[19] In London the government was only interested in success. The ill-prepared scheme of a Venezuelan revolutionary was one thing. The capture of Buenos Aires, unauthorised though it was, by a British expedition on 27 June 1806 was another. And while the admiralty rejected the argument of its commander, Sir Home Popham, that the operation was sanctioned by his previous negotiations with Pitt, political and commercial opinion in Britain reacted warmly to his resounding, if temporary, success. Miranda on the other hand could hardly contain his fury as he saw his 15 years of negotiations for independence ignored while Popham's instant conquest tempted the government into connivance.

Yet disaster at Coro acted as a spur to Miranda. In the West Indies he had made contact with a number of supporters among the British authorities, notably Admiral Alexander Cochrane and Governor Thomas Hislop. On his return to London he was welcomed by press and public with sympathy and support as someone who had at least struck a blow against the national enemies, while the government was criticised for its failure to support Miranda with men and ships. In Parliament Castlereagh rebuked the ministers' indecision over the expedition: 'We had sufficient force in the West Indies to have assisted General Miranda', but lack of instructions lost Britain important advantages. The government, anxious to find a chink in France's armour, was now looking seriously at South America. Miranda was received by ministers 'with friendship and attention, listening to my affairs with interest

19 Quoted by C. Parra Pérez, *Historia de la Primera República* (2 vols., Caracas, 1959), vol. I, pp. 262–3.

and concern'.[20] Castlereagh consulted Sir Arthur Wellesley, who had never liked the idea of stirring up social revolution for political reasons but now came out explicitly in favour of action, not for conquest but for independence: 'From what has lately passed at Buenos Ayres and from all that I have read of these countries, I am convinced that any attempt to conquer them, with a view to their future subjection to the British Crown, would certainly fail.' He saw no alternative to an independent regime, endowed with a monarchy and a manageable legislature, with suffrage based on age and property qualifications. The target for British action, he advised, should be first Mexico, then Venezuela.[21]

Miranda added his voice to a growing chorus, believing that now at last, with a government favourably disposed towards emancipation, his goal was in sight.[22] He was consulted frequently by Sir Arthur Wellesley; and he spoke earnestly to his friend Lord Melville, who recommended his project to Castlereagh at the war office. At this point he could see no major obstacle to British intervention in Spanish America. The danger from French ideology was regarded as a thing of the past. The issue of conquest versus independence seemed to have been resolved. The continental blockade imposed by Napoleon made the commercial argument more powerful than ever. By May 1808, with a French army in Madrid and the Spanish monarchy in collapse, Spain seemed lost beyond recall. Castlereagh now advised the government that it should take immediate steps to prevent the Spanish colonies from suffering the same fate as Spain itself, and at last he had an attentive audience.[23] On 4 May 1808 Miranda was invited to a meeting with Sir Arthur Wellesley, who informed him that the government had resolved to go ahead with his project: 'the thing is ultimately decided, according to our wishes', he wrote to Admiral Cochrane.[24] It was decided to assemble an expedi-

20 Miranda to Cochrane, 7 January 1808, *Archivo Miranda*, vol. XX, pp. 390–1; for Miranda's Memorandum to Castlereagh, 10 January 1808, see *ibid.*, vol. XXI, pp. 18–35, and Charles W. Vane, *Correspondence, Despatches, and Other Papers of Viscount Castlereagh* (12 vols., London, 1848–53), vol. VII, pp. 405–12.

21 Lynch, 'British Policy and Spanish America,' pp. 3, 22.

22 Miranda to Melville, 17 March 1808, NLS, Melville Mss W.L.C.L.

23 *Castlereagh Papers*, vol. VI, pp. 365–67.

24 Wellesley to Miranda, 4 May, Miranda to Cochrane, 5 May 1808, *Archivo Miranda*, vol. XXI, pp. 148, 154–5.

tionary force at Cork to attack Spanish America, and by 1 June its commander, Sir Arthur Wellesley, was making preparations for its departure. He was instructed to join General Spencer's force near Cadiz, and if circumstances were not propitious for intervention in the peninsula the joint force was to proceed to attack Spanish America. The exact destination of the expedition cannot be determined nor whether undiluted independence was the message it carried. These uncertainties can never be resolved, for the final orders were not given.[25]

Miranda held his breath: he knew that in Spain the rising of 2 May signified serious resistance to the French invaders and that in Britain the government was torn between priorities — action in Spain or in Spanish America? His correspondence in these weeks was an agonising exercise in persuasion as he mounted a last desperate assault upon the government, reaching for every possible argument to save the one project that gave meaning to his life. A diary entry at this time recorded a dinner and talk of 'nuestra América' with two army generals, 'enemigos siempre', he added bitterly, 'de su independencia!!'[26] As ministers struggled to make sense of the news from Spain and to satisfy Spanish demands, Miranda became an irritant and his project an irrelevance. It was made clear to him (though not by Vansittart) that the world had changed.

The Spanish uprising against the French invaders transformed the situation and removed one of the major pre-conditions of British intervention in Spanish America. Wellesley's expedition, therefore, sailed not to secure the independence of Spanish America but to restore the independence of Spain. There was a strategic logic in this decision which was difficult to resist. But Miranda did not give up the struggle or abandon the argument. He recorded in his diary an interview with Sir Arthur Wellesley on 26 January 1809, while the commander was on a visit from the peninsula:

> Today I had a long conference with Sir A. Wellesley, at his own request. I showed him all my correspondence with our Americas

25 For the sequence of events in 1808 see Roberston, *Life of Miranda*, vol. II, pp. 1–27.

26 Miranda to Castlereagh, 16 May, to Wellesley, 25 May, to Perceval, 26 May, to Canning, 26 May 1808, *Archivo Miranda*, vol. XXI, pp. 167–8, 176, 177–8, 191; *Diary*, 28 May 1808, *ibid.*, vol. XXI, pp. 175–6.

> and other papers carefully translated into English. I thought he read them with much care, attention and interest; he asked me not to speak to him while he was reading so as not to distract him. When he had finished he said to me calmly and quietly, I can only tell you this in friendship and confidence: at the moment the Ministry does not have its eyes on South America, and so I think it better to leave that subject until the Spanish business is concluded. — Well, I replied, do you not agree that England's attempt and plans to secure Independence in the Iberian Peninsula are already frustrated? — Yes, he replied, but we cannot deal with persons who come here from the Spanish colonies without failing the Spaniards and dishonouring ourselves … For the Spaniards would always say to us that if we were to protect the independence of their Americas it would be better for them to treat with France — Then to deal with me would be even more incompatible than to deal with anyone else? — No, he replied, for I have an express order from His Majesty's ministers to receive whatever communications you may judge convenient in these matters but neither to communicate with nor to receive any other person. He proceeded immediately to ask my opinion about the public spirit of the continental Spanish American colonies, supposing that Spain declared for Joseph Bonaparte. On learning that I believed that the majority would favour *Absolute Independence*, he promptly replied, Well, that is what we desire too! And as for *Government, that is their business*, not England's … He assured me that he would always be happy to see me, and once the Spanish business was over, *which he did not believe would be long*, then we would turn all our attention to America! And so I took my leave.

The interview with Wellesley made a strong impression on Miranda. He believed that it revealed the English government's real intentions on Spanish America. His diary entry concludes with his own analysis:

> 1st — As soon as the Spaniards proposed an alliance against France, at that moment they abandoned us and sacrificed their own interests without the slightest regret. 2nd — When they perceived that we desired to be independent of the French, they then affected an indifference, in order to sell their friendship or protec-

> tion as dearly as possible. 3rd — Observing that Spanish America does not lend itself to guidance and influence in matters of *Government and Commerce*, they wish to show indifference as to the form of Government that is chosen for the country — unless it is that of Ferdinand VII, their worthy Ally.[27]

Miranda never accepted the validity of the choice of Spain over America or appreciated the deference shown by Britain to its crumbling ally, but he now knew that he could not alter British foreign policy and that the desired object of his long sojourn in England was unattainable. He could not restrain his incomprehension, as he revealed in a letter to Castlereagh:

> It is surprising to me that a plan of this importance, and so essentially connected with the interests of this country should have been upon the point of execution by a series of administrations from the year 1790, beginning with Mr. Pitt; zealously adopted by Lord Sidmouth and St. Vincent; resumed by Mr. Pitt and Lord Melville and ultimately embraced by Your Lordship and your colleagues, by some fatality unaccountable to me, have as frequently been defeated.[28]

For Miranda the reversal of alliances was a reversal of his own status: in the eyes of Britain's new ally he was a traitor and a rebel. For his remaining two years in London, marginalised from the government yet with a reputation enhanced by his long dedication to a liberal cause and negotiations with successive administrations, he focused on propaganda not politics.

Ideas and their Authors

Miranda was educated in the classics of Greece and Rome, but above all he was a man of the eighteenth century, whose mind was informed not by traditional theology or scholasticism but by the *philosophes* and deists of contemporary France: Montesquieu, Voltaire, Rousseau, Raynal, and the

27 Miranda, *Diary*, 26 January 1809, *Archivo Miranda*, vol. XXII, pp. 208–10.

28 Miranda to Castlereagh, 24 March 1809, *Archivo Miranda*, vol. XXII, pp. 246–50.

historians and political economists of Scotland and England. Miranda's guiding text was the *Grande Encyclopédie* of Diderot and D'Alembert whose 36 volumes in the 1781 edition he had in his library. Miranda spoke the language of natural rights and took it for granted that liberty and equality were absolute values discernable by human reason. In religion he was a deist, though he accepted the Catholic Church as part of society. He wanted his son Leander 'to be baptised by a Priest of the Roman Church, but quietly and with the agreement of his mother'.[29] His scheme of provisional government for Spanish America stated that, 'The Roman Catholic religion will be the national religion, and the hierarchy of American clergy will be regulated by a provincial council.' The document recognised the pope as head of the Church but insisted on religious toleration and abolition of the 'odious Inquisition'.[30] Miranda was at bottom anticlerical (the Jesuits excepted), antipapal and anti-Catholic; he visited churches and attended services wherever he was and whatever the cult, but for social rather than religious reasons, and sometimes simply to look at women. His European travel writings contain stereotypes. Catholic regions are full of beggars, poverty and squalor, with friars preaching damnation, while Protestants are associated with prosperity and progress: 'the same country, the same climate, but one is free, the other not'. 'May we not conclude that in Catholicism there is something opposed to public prosperity?'[31]

Miranda never stopped writing, but his ideas were not systematically developed or expressed and he left nothing comparable to Juan Pablo Viscardo's *Letter to Spanish Americans* or Simón Bolívar's *Jamaica Letter*.[32] Historians can reconstruct his thought from the thousands of letters, occasional writings and the incomparable Diary; these are collected in

29 Miranda to Turnbull, New York, 4 January 1806, *Archivo Miranda*, vol. XVII, p. 332.

30 *Ibid.*, vol. XVI, pp. 133, 152, 159.

31 *Diario de Suiza*, 4, 8, 9, 17 August 1788, *Colombeia*, vol. VII, pp. 388–9, 397–8, 399, 410; Lautico García, *Francisco de Miranda y el Antiguo Regimen Español* (Caracas, 1961), pp. 395–417.

32 See Juan Pablo Viscardo y Guzman, 'Letter to the Spanish Americans,' translated by James Mill writing as William Burke, in William Burke, *Additional Reasons for Immediately Emancipating Spanish America* (London, 1808), pp. 95–124; and Simón Bolívar, *Selected Writings*, compiled by Vicente Lecuna, edited by Harold A. Bierck, Jr., translation by Lewis Bertrand, 2 vols. (New York, 1951), vol. 1, p. 105.

the 24 volumes of the *Archivo de Miranda*, destined to be superseded by the monumental *Colombeia*, which Venezuelan editors are in the process of assembling from the 63 folio volumes of the Miranda Manuscripts and other sources. An additional problem arises from the fact that in England much of Miranda's thought was published under the names of other authors, and one of these authors further hid his identity behind a pseudonym. William Burke, the so-called journalist from Dublin and collaborator of Miranda, did not exist. Mario Rodríguez shows conclusively that 'William Burke' was not an obscure Irish author but a distinguished Scottish philosopher and historian, James Mill, alumnus of the University of Edinburgh, product of the Scottish Enlightenment, collaborator of Jeremy Bentham and father of John Stuart Mill. James Mill was the jewel in the crown of Miranda's intellectual circle.[33]

Miranda's modesty as an author in London was due to his determination to protect his reputation as a serious negotiator, who could be trusted with confidences by the statesmen with whom he dealt, a reputation which would be damaged if he acted as a journalist and propagandist. At the same time there were years when his great enemy Spain was an ally or at least at peace with Britain and he would risk censure or even expulsion if the Spaniards protested at his activities. For more or less the same reasons James Mill, a young writer still making his way, whose utilitarian writings and *History of India* lay ahead of him, did not wish to arouse the ire of English governments which were not famous for tolerating a hostile press.

Miranda's basic doctrine, in which Spain's policy in America is compared to a two-edged sword, received early expression in an article in the *Political Herald and Review* in 1785, probably written by one of his friends:

> The flame which was kindled in North America, as was foreseen, has made its way into the American dominions of Spain. That jealousy which confined the appointments of government in Spanish America to native Spaniards, and established other distinctions between these and their descendants on the other side of the Atlantic, has been a two-edged sword and cuts two ways. If it has hitherto preserved the sovereignty of Spain in those parts, it has sown the seeds of a deep resentment among the people.[34]

33 Rodríguez, '*William Burke*' *and Francisco de Miranda*, pp. 58–9, 123–53.

34 *Ibid.*, p. 11; see above, note 4.

This was the continuing message of Miranda to his English audience: Spanish colonial control was oppressive, it denied power and representation to Spanish Americans, who now had before their eyes the example of the United States. There were longer or shorter versions of the argument, with greater or less historical detail, but the essence remained. The example of the United States was a compelling idea for Miranda. He also insisted that action in the Americas was a better option for Britain than coalitions in Europe. 'A few prudent steps' on Britain's part would bring advantages for South America and benefits for Britain.[35]

Miranda appealed to those, such as James Mill, who advocated an alternative foreign policy. The enemy was France, of which Spain was frequently an ally or a satellite. Mill was convinced that Britain blundered in seeking collaboration with Spain rather than action in Spanish America. The objective should be emancipation, not plunder: 'the same advantages which we have reaped from the independence of the Northern part of the Continent we may derive by propagating a spirit of independence in the South'.[36] The rewards included new commercial opportunities once the Spanish colonial monopoly had been broken. Views of this kind point to the existence of a dissenting foreign policy in England to which Miranda could appeal; he was not a lone voice crying unheard. The British government itself was aware of the Spanish colonies. Travellers who had gained entry to South America, merchants who had traded on its coasts, naval and official personnel in the West Indies, all these provided ministers with a working knowledge of conditions in the subcontinent, sometimes in circumstantial detail. One of the most prolific sources of information, outside Miranda's team, was William Jacob, FRS, economist and merchant, who had traded for some years to Spanish America and who volunteered to the government a number of plans for liberating expeditions and consequent commercial opportunities.[37] These plans, however, languished in the archives. Miranda sought the light of day.

35 Antepara, *South American Emancipation*, pp. 7–8.

36 Quoted by Rodríguez, *'William Burke' and Francisco de Miranda*, p. 223.

37 Memorials by Jacob, 26 October 1804, 14 February 1809 [1806], 1 August 1811, National Archive (NA), Chatham Papers, G.D. 8/345, FO 72/90, FO 72/122. Jacob considered Miranda a dangerous extremist, given to 'the wildest flights of democracy'.

In 1807–08 the argument was raised to a higher level in two pamphlets by James Mill, writing under the name of William Burke. The first of these, *South American Independence*, was written by Mill on his own initiative and from his own research, and begun in about 1803 before he made direct contact with Miranda.[38] Spanish rule in America, he argued, was based on bloody conquest and violent possession; it was unjust and tyrannical, an affront to natural rights. The Spaniards had broken the principles of strict justice for the Indians by their arbitrary behaviour and had lost their legitimacy through their record of oppression. Americans therefore 'derive their rights to their country and independence, from the best of all titles, nature and justice'.[39] Mill's description of social and economic conditions under Spanish colonial rule is coloured by national prejudice and his conclusion is typically assertive: 'God, who created America, made it for the benefit of its people: and has given them a right and power to possess and enjoy their country, free from the intrusion and interference of lawless invaders.'[40] Other nations too have their rights infringed by Spain's determination to enforce a monopoly of wealth and trade. Spain 'by hermetically sealing up her immense possessions in America from the rest of the world, excepting her own stupid despotism; commits an injustice against other nations, which it is both their duty and interest immediately to destroy.'[41] Britain had a right and an interest to intervene in favour of independence in order to share in the resources of America and profit from its trade. In the 'glorious work' of liberating America we will serve the world and 'serve ourselves, by opening new, rich, and numerous markets for the sale of our manufactures, and by cutting off from our present powerful adversary the important resources which he derives from Spain possessing America'. These interests will best be served by a policy of emancipation, not conquest, which would be counterproductive.[42] Policy and justice go hand in hand. Spanish Americans are ready for liberty. 'This melioration in the colonial mind', concluded Mill, precipitated by the American and

38 *South American Independence: or, the Emancipation of South America, the Glory and Interest of England* (London, 1807).

39 *Ibid.*, p. 9.

40 *Ibid.*, p. 13.

41 *Ibid.*, p. 15.

42 *Ibid.*, pp. 21–2, 28–33.

French Revolutions, is a powerful force for change. 'General Miranda … is a proud and illustrious proof, that Southern Colombia has sons, who can and do estimate the blessings of liberty, like other men.'[43]

Miranda received a copy of Mill's pamphlet in July 1807 while still in the West Indies, and immediately identified the author as a valuable ally, one who would bring intellectual quality to the cause of emancipation. He hoped that it would open the eyes of the British public: 'It appears that even the Public Mind perceives now, what was sound Policy and Interest of Great Britain to have executed a long time ago.'[44] For the second paper Mill had access to Miranda's library and indirectly to his advice, reflected in the details he could give of the Venezuelan and his country, and also in the decision to publish as an Appendix the 'Letter to the Spanish Americans' by Juan Pablo Viscardo y Guzmán, an English translation of 'this valuable little tract … which does equal honour to the writer, as an enlightened patriot, politician and Christian'.[45]

The second paper takes up the concluding argument of the first. The ruinous and inglorious attempt to take Spanish America by force had failed in the Río de la Plata because Britain had sought conquest, not independence. Unfortunately public censure was being directed exclusively against General Whitelocke, not against the policy makers. Blockaded in the old world, Britain could find raw materials and export markets in the new: Spanish America 'requires of us but to employ the master-key of independence, to unlock her treasures to our use'. Miranda offered a superior model in his expedition to Venezuela, but this too had failed, because it lacked the military edge which even slight British support could have supplied. The time had come for Britain to respond to the 'rapidly rising views of national independence'.[46] Mill's eloquence soared. 'A great colonial revolution appears to me to be on the eve of taking place; and which, if we do not in time adopt necessary and commensurate measures for taking it under our auspices and

43 *Ibid.*, pp. 65–7.

44 Miranda to Vansittart, 11 July, to Cochrane, 22 July 1807, *Archivo Miranda*, vol. XIX, pp. 104–5.

45 William Burke, *Additional Reasons for Our Immediately Emancipating Spanish America* (2nd edition, London, 1808); see Rodríguez, '*William Burke*' *and Francisco de Miranda*, pp. 160–1.

46 Burke, *Additional Reasons*, pp. 16–18, 32, 33–4, 52–3.

direction, might be made to operate to our disadvantage.'[47] The arguments bore the imprint of Miranda, who on his return to London promptly made contact with his new ally and began the distribution of the work to friends and institutions outside England.

The alliance of Britain and Spain in June 1808 forced Miranda to accept defeat on the political front. He now changed tactics. Discarding discretion, he embarked on a campaign of propaganda in open collaboration with James Mill.[48] Mill was ready to risk his own prospects through the opportunity of publishing in the leading intellectual journal of the time, *The Edinburgh Review*, a medium known to be open to South American subjects. The result was two celebrated articles, in which Mill supplied the writing, structure and knowledge of reader interests, and Miranda the specialist evidence. The first, published in January 1809 under the title 'Emancipation of Spanish America' was a 34 page essay, which began with a favourable review of Viscardo's *Letter to Spanish Americans* and then proceeded to develop a series of reasoned arguments in favour of independence.[49] These opened with a direct appeal to British interests, using Mill's expert knowledge of the economic case for British intervention and his awareness of 'the prejudices of this nation'.[50] There were 'brilliant prospects' awaiting at a time when Napoleon dominated the continent and Britain needed new commercial outlets. Here was a vast market for British manufactures and a source of vital raw materials, more promising even than the North American market. Such advantages, however, would only be secured by a policy of liberation, not conquest, thus avoiding the catastrophe of British intervention in the Río de la Plata in 1806–07. Mill asked whether England should undertake the conquest of South America for itself. No one contemplates such a thing, and in any case it would not be an easy conquest. 'We mention this idea, therefore, only for the purpose of setting it aside.'[51]

47 *Ibid.*, p. 87.

48 On Miranda as a propagandist see Robertson, *Life of Miranda*, vol. II, pp. 28–70; María Teresa Berruezo León, *La lucha de Hispanoamérica por su independencia en Inglaterra, 1800–1830* (Madrid, 1989), pp. 49–75; Rodríguez, '*William Burke' and Francisco de Miranda*, pp. 201–42.

49 *The Edinburgh Review*, vol. XIII, no. 26 (January 1809), pp. 277–311.

50 Mill to Miranda, 4 January 1809, *Archivo Miranda*, vol. XXII, pp. 183, 184.

51 *The Edinburgh Review*, January 1809, pp. 279–80, 299.

The article proceeded with a carefully edited *curriculum vitae* of Miranda, one likely to appeal to English readers who would note his stand against the Jacobins in France, culminating in the reversal of alliances with Spain and the British decision to abandon the Spanish American project. Yet Britain could still proceed, if it had the will, leaving the ultimate form of government in Spanish America to its own people. But not to all the people. Both Mill and Miranda showed a decided aversion to popular revolution. Miranda himself had observed in 1799, affected no doubt by his own tribulations in France, 'We have before our eyes two great examples, the American and the French Revolutions. Let us prudently imitate the first and carefully shun the fatal effects of the second.'[52] Now with Mill he argued, 'The people — whose ignorance and irritability may be worked upon by men of evil intentions, require, in the crisis of any political change, the most sage precautions — are never called upon for their interference. They remain at their homes.'[53] Another version of the supposed motto of enlightened despotism, 'Everything for the people, nothing by the people.' In the context of social stability, the article further argued that representation could best be provided by the traditional institutions of *cabildos* and provincial assemblies, elected by all inhabitants, with a national assembly elected by the *cabildo* alone. The executive would be Miranda's favoured Inca, a monarchical form of government which Mill thought to be 'dear to South America'. As for the judiciary, Jeremy Bentham was 'the man, unquestionably, of all who have ever lived, by far the best qualified to give advice on this subject'.[54] Mill and Miranda were aware that in advocating British intervention in Spanish America at a time when Britain supported the imperial integrity of its ally they were risking government displeasure. Mill, self-assured by nature, was unperturbed. He insisted that he was simply engaged in 'interesting the nation at large in a project which has hitherto been almost exclusively the nurseling of ministers; and thus binding the government to more prompt and effectual exertions in behalf of a cause which may have become popular as well as important'.[55] The article survived editorial scrutiny and was published as it stood.

52 Miranda to Manuel Gual, 31 December 1799, *Archivo Miranda*, vol. XV, p. 404.

53 *The Edinburgh Review*, January 1809, pp. 304–5.

54 *Ibid.*, pp. 308–9.

55 *Ibid.*, p. 311; see also *Archivo Miranda*, vol. XXII, pp. 189–90, 193–4.

In July of the same year Miranda collaborated with Mill on a second article in *The Edinburgh Review*, which followed the lines of the first, strengthened the argument and supplied further evidence.[56] Like the first, it introduced a Jesuit author, this time Juan Ignacio Molina, whose two volumes on Chile were reviewed sympathetically to increase British knowledge of Spanish America and to lead into a powerfully argued case for Spanish American emancipation, 'an event to be numbered among the greatest which the course of human affairs could bring forth'.[57] The opportunity for Britain was again underlined: to destroy the Spanish monopoly was to open up a vast and fertile continent to the benefits of free trade. In an eloquent and focused argument, researched in Miranda's library from Francisco Javier Clavijero and other authorities, Mill sketched for the reader a historical geography of Spanish America and a quantification of the economic benefits of emancipation. Guided no doubt by Miranda, he saw through the sham of a Spanish national Cortes with representation for Spanish America. On any equitable distribution of seats the Spanish American representatives would be nearly twice as numerous as those from Spain itself. 'The representatives from South America become the governor of Spain, and South America is the metropolitan country.' Spaniards would not accept this and the result would be civil war.[58] Finally, the article outlined for Britain a Spanish American policy. The treaty of alliance with Spain was dismissed as a trap for Britain. If it meant guaranteeing the integrity of the Spanish empire, it was both impolitic and impossible to apply, because all the forces of Britain would be insufficient for such a purpose. 'Could we, if we were mad enough to stake Great Britain upon the contest, prevent the independence of South America, if South America were resolved to be independent?' To tie Britain's hands in this way 'was an instance of misconduct among the grossest to be found in the huge library of ministerial imbecilities'.[59] Miranda could think this; only Mill could say it.

At the same time as he was addressing the British media through Mill and other collaborators, Miranda was exporting a profusion of revolu-

56 *The Edinburgh Review*, vol. XIV, no. 28 (July, 1809), pp. 333–53.
57 *Ibid.*, p. 335.
58 *Ibid.*, p. 347.
59 *Ibid.*, pp. 346, 351.

tionary material to Spanish America with the help of British writers and publishers, and of his naval friends in the West Indies. Admiral Alexander Cochrane provided a virtual mail service for Miranda until he was stopped by his superiors in December 1808.[60] Through one channel or another Miranda was able to reach the *cabildos* of Caracas, Buenos Aires, Mexico City and Cuba with his letters and copies of propaganda materials. As the Spanish government and its war effort fell apart, so Miranda questioned the legitimacy of authorities in the peninsula and urged his compatriots in America to prepare for the day of separation. Spanish officials reacted angrily in America and in Europe, and during a casual meeting with Miranda in London Castlereagh lectured him that British ministers 'were not too happy with you maintaining so much correspondence with the provinces of South America — while at the same time receiving a salary from this government'.[61]

One of Miranda's principal weapons of propaganda was Juan Pablo Viscardo's *Lettre aux Espagnols Américains*, first published by Miranda in 1799 and quickly recognised as a classic statement of colonial grievance and the case for independence. Three dominant arguments developed by the Peruvian former Jesuit appealed to Miranda. First, the factor of distance and concept of *patria*: separated from Spain by nature, Americans were even more separated by interests. Second, the favour shown to peninsular Spaniards over creoles in appointments: this was a reversal of earlier policy and a denial of the right of Americans to govern themselves. Third, the tyranny exercised by Spain: Americans were deprived of liberty and equality, exploited economically and deprived of political control. Miranda had the *Letter* translated into Spanish for circulation in Spanish America before and during his expedition to Venezuela, and in the years after his return from Coro he made it the leading weapon in his war of words.

By 1810 it was clear that the Anglo-Spanish alliance was holding and there would be no British help for the American project. Miranda decided he had nothing to lose and now fired further rounds of propaganda targeted on Spanish America but also intended to educate 'the thinking part of the British people' in the realities of the Hispanic world.[62]

60 Rodríguez, '*William Burke*' *and Francisco de Miranda*, pp. 182, 197–9.

61 Miranda, *Diary*, 24 April 1809, *Archivo Miranda*, vol. XXI, p. 301.

62 Burke, *South American Emancipation*, p. 7.

His principal medium was *El Colombiano*, of which he published five numbers between 15 March and 15 May 1810.[63] Edited nominally by José María Antepara, supervised by James Mill and financed by Mexican creoles, the periodical was the voice of Miranda and spoke his basic thoughts. Miranda's friend Nicholas Vansittart was perturbed: 'if I had been in town I should have advised against such a publication — as it will require extraordinary caution to avoid exciting jealousies and giving a handle to your enemies.'[64] The title itself was a Miranda concept, his hallmark, projecting America as one great country, its people as a single community.

This was the most defiant of all Miranda's publications in London, an uninhibited attack on the two great enemies of Spanish American independence. First it expressed his hatred of Napoleon and his 'monstrous power', fired by his own humiliating experiences in France, the emperor's refusal to assist his project and the danger of French penetration in Spanish America. Second, and even more bitterly, it mounted a sustained attack on England's ally Spain, in particular on the Junta Central, the Regency and other organs of what Miranda regarded as Spain's pseudo-resistance. These false institutions lacked legality and were sufficient reasons in themselves — apart from Spain's malign record in America — to justify America's claim to independence. As for the Cortes, they were utterly unrepresentative of the Americas which 'by reason of their population and wealth are infinitely superior to Spain'.[65] If English critics of Spanish government such as Sir John Moore and the Marquis of Wellesley questioned its legitimacy and condemned its incompetence, why should Spanish Americans accept it?[66] Spain in default of a real government and a free king had become an extension of the Napoleonic empire. Miranda encouraged input from Blanco White, who contributed a Spanish liberal viewpoint. Finally, *El Colombiano* published the 'Thoughts of an Englishman on the State and Present Crisis of Affairs in South America' by James Mill, a forthright restatement of his articles in *The Edinburgh Review* and an indictment of three centuries of 'vilest servitude' which fed American desire for emancipation and good government. 'The

63 Francisco de Miranda, *El Colombiano*, Prólogo C. Parra Pérez, Nota bibliográfica Pedro Grases (Caracas, 1952).

64 Vansittart to Miranda, 20 April 1810, *Archivo Miranda*, vol. XXIII, p. 405.

65 *El Colombiano*, p. 3.

66 *Ibid.*, pp. 33–4.

inhabitants of the New World are called, by the voice of God and of men, to form a government by themselves and for themselves', he concluded, but if they want to be truly free they must give priority to '*security of the person and of property*'.[67]

El Colombiano was always going to be a high-risk publication. The British government took the Spanish alliance seriously and paid attention to complaints of Spanish representatives in London. The anti-Napoleonic stance of the periodical counted for nothing. Miranda had been warned more than once that the propaganda campaign which he carried directly into Spanish America was seditious in Spanish eyes, and Castlereagh had informed him 'that if he continues an intercourse inconsistent with H.M.'s relations with Spain, he will be expelled'.[68] Now it was made clear that further attacks on Britain's ally would certainly bring about his expulsion. He closed down *El Colombiano* after the issue of 15 May 1810.

If the news from Spain incensed him, that from Venezuela raised his hopes. On 19 April 1810 revolutionaries in Caracas deposed and deported the Spanish administration and established an independent junta to govern Venezuela. Miranda had the details by late June and soon he was occupied with the Venezuelan mission to London and then with his own departure from a city which had been his home for 14 years.

Nerve Centre of Independence

Miranda's London home was the first stop for Spanish Americans visiting England in the years from 1797, not simply for contacts but for advice and ideas. Robertson writes: 'Among the important results of Miranda's residence in London were the significant affiliations that he formed with those Spanish Americans who made his residence a meeting place.'[69] Antonio Nariño, Pedro Fermín de Vargas, Pedro José Caro and other itinerants were all indebted to him in one way or another: in some cases he simply strengthened their existing beliefs, in others he implanted new ideas. Bernardo O'Higgins spoke in 1811 of 'how I was converted to the doctrines of that intelligent and tireless apostle of the

67 *Ibid.*, pp. 45–6, 59.

68 Cooke to Hammond, 22 May 1809, NA, FO 72/90.

69 Robertson, *Life of Miranda*, vol. I, p. 211.

cause of South America'.[70] The doctrines were independence, liberty and unity, the three great causes for which Miranda stood throughout his public life. In 1810 in a circular letter to Spanish Americans he wrote: 'My house in this city is the fixed point for the independence and liberties of the Colombian continent, and it always will be.'[71] From 1802 that house was 27 Grafton Street (now 58 Grafton Way) and it served not only as a home for Miranda, his companion, Sarah Andrews, his two sons, Leander and Francisco, and his secretary, Tomás Molini and his wife, but also as a resource centre for Latin American studies. As such it housed his library, seminar rooms, the editorial offices of *El Colombiano* and lodgings for a select group of Spanish Americans in the summer of 1810.[72]

These were the delegates from Venezuela, Simón Bolívar, Luis López Méndez and Andrés Bello, who arrived in early July in search of British support for the revolutionary movement in Caracas. They had been warned by the Caracas junta to beware of Miranda who was suspect to some creoles as a French Revolutionary extremist, but in the event they would have been nothing without Miranda. According to López Méndez the delegation arrived in London lost and disorientated, and it was Miranda who rescued them from oblivion:

> The only person we could consult with confidence and who could give us the preliminary briefings we needed was our compatriot; he more than anyone else, with his extensive experience and travels, his long contacts with this government and his well known exertions for America, was in a position to give us wide and reliable advice. Even his enemies have never dared to deny his extraordinary knowledge, experience and talents. He was extremely helpful to us and placed his knowledge, his books, his influence and his contacts completely at our disposal.[73]

70 Quoted by Berruezo, *La lucha de Hispanoamérica*, p. 39.

71 Miranda, Circular letter to 'nuestras Américas', 24 March 1810, *Archivo Miranda*, vol. XXIII, pp. 367–8.

72 José Luis Salcedo-Bastardo, *Crisol del americanismo: la casa de Miranda en Londres* (Caracas, 1980). Number 58 Grafton Way is named Miranda House, and it contains the Venezuelan Embassy's cultural office and library.

73 López Méndez to Venezuelan secretary of state, London, 3 October 1810, quoted by Berruezo, *La lucha de Hispanoamérica*, pp. 91–2.

Andrés Bello was equally impressed: 'That great exile personified in himself the Spanish American revolution. He was already 60 years old. But in spite of his age he seemed to be at the height of his youth and ideals, and he persisted in all the plans for promoting the independence of Spanish America, never losing hope of seeing this desire fulfilled.'[74] Bolívar, according to his aide-de-camp Daniel Florencio O'Leary, eager no doubt to put the best gloss on the Liberator's relations with Miranda, 'had long recognised in Miranda not only great military genius but also the veteran who had been the first to try and rescue Venezuela from oppression. He believed that … he had discovered in Miranda the man whose happy destiny reserved for him the glory of realising the splendid project of emancipating South America.' Bolívar urged Miranda to return to Venezuela to serve the cause 'for which he had suffered so much'.[75]

More immediately Miranda spent hours arranging meetings and interviews for the delegates and briefing them in appropriate arguments, introducing them to significant institutions such as Joseph Lancaster's school in Borough Road, as well as taking them to the tourist sights of London, Greenwich and Richmond. Independence was the agenda that Miranda urged them to follow in their negotiations, rather than loyalty to Ferdinand which they had been instructed to invoke. But British support was a lost cause and the Venezuelans could make no impression on the foreign minister, the Marquis of Wellesley. Miranda knew the situation from memory.

Britain was in a difficult position: the war in the peninsula was at a critical conjuncture and Wellesley would not risk offending Spain by recognising the new Venezuelan government. Nor did he wish to offend the Venezuelans by refusing to receive the mission, for they could soon be independent of Spain. In any case there were commercial advantages at stake: the foreign office thought that 'by use of the bond of allegiance to Ferdinand England may preserve her colonies to Spain yet compel Spain to alter her commercial system'.[76] He therefore decided to receive

74 Quoted by José Luis Salcedo-Bastardo, 'Bello and the "Symposiums" of Grafton Street,' in John Lynch (ed.), *Andrés Bello: The London Years* (Richmond, 1982), p. 63.

75 *Memorias del General O'Leary* (Ministerio de la Defensa, 27–28, 2 vols., Caracas, 1981), vol. I, p. 34.

76 Notes on the Caraccas, 5 August 1810, NA, FO 72/106.

the Venezuelans privately at his home; hence the meetings at Apsley House. At the first meeting, on 16 July, the delegates made their position clear: the Spanish regency was illegal and unacceptable. Wellesley insisted that to reject the regency was to declare independence, which Britain regarded as incompatible with the Anglo-Spanish alliance. The deadlock was never resolved, in spite of further meetings. The Venezuelans sought to reassure the Foreign Office that theirs was not an extremist movement: 'the deputies say there was little expression of popular feeling in the revolution, the people of all castes being in total ignorance were easily led.'[77] But it appeared that Britain was more concerned to satisfy Spain than to influence Venezuela, though it did not act against the government in Caracas or eject its agents, two of whom, López Méndez and Andrés Bello, remained in London to speak for Venezuela.[78] Bolívar left England on 22 September in a vessel of the royal navy. Miranda, too, wanted to sail in this and he even loaded his luggage and 63 volumes of documents on board, but the British government was reluctant to provoke Spain and the vessel left without him.

The outbreak of revolution in Venezuela and the arrival of its delegates brought an end to Miranda's mission in London. On 25 July he made his first request to Wellesley for authorisation to leave, thanking the British government 'not only for the friendship and generosity, with which they have supported me for the space of more than twenty years of an intimate connexion, in affairs of the greatest importance and in the most eventful times — but for the Hospitality and approbation shewn to me, by the various administrations.'[79] The irony, conscious or not, survived to the bitter end, for the foreign minister dragged his feet, as the British government had done for 20 years, still willing to protect Spain from its famous revolutionary. Further letters followed but Miranda was left waiting. Finally, on 3 October, he informed Wellesley that he was going anyway, and on 10 October, accompanied by Molini but without his family, he sailed on a packet boat. He reached La Guaira on 11 December.

77 *Ibid.*

78 D.A.G. Waddell, *Gran Bretaña y la Independencia de Venezuela y Colombia* (Caracas, 1983), pp. 64–72.

79 Miranda to Wellesley, 25 July 1810, *Archivo Miranda*, vol. XXIII, pp. 476–8; further letters, NA, FO 72/171.

While Miranda and Bolívar went to war Bello took advantage of the free lodgings in Grafton Street to study in Miranda's library and there to learn Greek, 'the medium of a great literature'. Politicians, intellectuals and journalists in London also benefited from that great library in their midst, significant not only for its size but also for its inclusiveness: 6,000 books in virtually all disciplines — history, military studies, politics, American studies, literature from classical to modern, art and architecture, music, the sciences.[80] London was the base where the library was formed; much of it was collected on his diverse travels, but as he purchased from dealers and bookshops in the Americas and Europe so he sent the books to his home in England, where they joined those he bought in London. It became one of the best libraries in London, almost a lending library for the liberal and radical intellectuals of the time. William Wilberforce, Joseph Lancaster, James Mill, Jeremy Bentham, the scholar William Thomson, all used and borrowed from Miranda's collection. As Pi Sunyer comments, you may argue about the life and ideas of Miranda, as people did and do: he was a controversial character who provoked reactions. But one thing cannot be denied: the quality of his library, not only its intrinsic value but also as a mirror of eighteenth-century culture and the personality of its owner.[81] It was also, of course, an economic asset, which he used as a surety for the debts incurred in his expedition to Venezuela in 1806, and after his death for the maintenance of his family. He bequeathed the 126 volumes of his classics collection to the University of Caracas. The remaining 5,600 volumes were sold in two auctions in London in 1828 and 1833, raising an unspectacular £1,125 sterling.

London Acclaim

Miranda had two specific achievements to his credit in London. First, he placed Spanish America and its independence on the map of contemporary history and educated the 'thinking part' of the British public in an area that Spain had sought to seal off from the rest of the world. Second, in the course of 20 years he persuaded the British government to take this

80 Arturo Uslar Pietri and Pedro Grases, *Los libros de Miranda* (Caracas, 1979), pp. xi–lxx.

81 Carlos Pi Sunyer, *Patriotas americanos en Londres* (Caracas, 1978), p. 57.

single issue as a serious subject of debate, if not of decision. His ultimate failure as a lobbyist was due not to infirmity of purpose on his part but to the limits imposed on British policy by its worldwide commitments.

It is true that there were question marks over Miranda. He could be mistaken for an adventurer, a deserter, a dilettante, a Casanova and (for British ministers at least) a persistent nuisance. His enemies in Spain, at the Spanish legation in London and in Venezuela denounced him as a traitor, a rebel and a freethinker. But among serious people in London he was known as a serious person, a professional soldier with battle experience, an expert source of information and advice, a committed Americanist and a good friend. The various ministers with whom he negotiated respected him and listened to him even if they did not respond. Melville and Vansittart were friends as well as supporters, providing invaluable information on English politics and access to higher levels. Pownall and Turnbull were special friends who helped him for many years and in particular ways; and in the West Indies Admiral Cochrane and Governor Hislop were important allies who were ready to come to his assistance. Among aristocratic friends he could number the Duke of Cumberland, the Duke of Gloucester, Richard Wellesley, son of the foreign minister, Lady Ann Townsend and Lady Hester Stanhope.

In addition to his Latin American expertise, the military credentials of Miranda, and the military holdings of his library, were held in high regard. The historian William Thomson consulted him extensively in the years around 1800 when he was researching for his book *Military Memoirs*. Thomson was also influenced by Miranda in his revision of the events of 1806–07 in the Río de la Plata; he altered his review of the history of that year in the *Annual Register* in favour of Miranda's concept of liberation as opposed to Popham's preference for conquest and corrected the errors circulating in London concerning Miranda's Venezuelan expedition in 1806.[82]

The London media, and London journalists, followed the opinions and activities of Miranda with keen interest, often no doubt prodded and primed by Miranda himself, who was good at public relations. But he aroused sympathy as well as interest. His expedition to Coro in 1806, marginalised or rebuffed by the British and United States governments,

82 Rodríguez, *'William Burke' and Francisco de Miranda*, pp. 175–9.

was amply reported in the London press. *The Times* published numerous articles and reports from sources in the United States, the British West Indies, Spain and France, and Miranda himself emerged with credit from an expedition which had failed in so many ways.[83]

The liberal and radical wing of English public life, of course, Wilberforce, Lancaster, Bentham, were reliable allies. Miranda expressed his admiration for 'those humane, Christian and philanthropic virtues' possessed by Wilberforce.[84] After returning to London in 1808 he renewed his acquaintance with Bentham, visiting him at his home, lending him books and unpublished papers and borrowing too from Bentham's library. The date of the first meeting between Mill and Bentham is not known, but following the article of January 1809 in *The Edinburgh Review,* Miranda seems to have become an early link between the two and influential in focusing their joint attention on Spanish American independence. Later in that year Bentham invited Miranda to join him and Mill in the country.[85] He continued to take a close interest in Miranda and his ideas and planned to remain in contact with him after his departure for Venezuela. 'He took with him the draft of a law which, at his solicitation, I drew up for the establishing of the liberty of the Press. He is to write to me immediately on his arrival; and if things are in a peaceable state, I shall probably take a trip thither not long after I have his letter.'[86] Although the trip was not possible, the ideas of Bentham flowed freely across the Atlantic and the principle of utility found eager disciples throughout the Americas.

James Mill was Miranda's closest friend and collaborator in London, drawn to the older man by his ideas, his experience and the cause which he served. Like Bentham, Mill saw Spanish American independence as

83 Turnbull to Miranda, 5 and 7 June 1806, NLS, Cochrane Papers 2320, f. 16; Vansittart to Windham, 22 January 1807, BL, Add. 37885, f. 231; Windham to Grenville, 11 September 1806, Historical Manuscripts Commission, *Dropmore Papers* (10 vols., London, 1892–1927), vol. VIII, p. 321.

84 Miranda to Wilberforce, 18 March 1809, *Archivo Miranda,* vol. XXII, p. 244, thanking him for the loan of books.

85 Bentham to Miranda, 25 August 1809, *The Correspondence of Jeremy Bentham, Volume 8, January 1809 to December 1816*, edited by Stephen Conway (Oxford, 1988), pp. 42–3.

86 Bentham to John Mulford, 1 November 1810; *ibid.*, vol. VIII, p. 77.

a model for applied liberalism, where principles could be tested and plans brought to life. Writing to Miranda in May 1809 to announce a visit to his house to discuss a matter of mutual interest, Mill requests

> As I shall dislike the idea, however, of parting again for the day, I hope you will have no objection to come on and dine with us. You need make no scruple of coming from any delicacy about putting us to trouble, for I ask nobody to dine at my frugal table whose taste I know is not as simple as my own, and who will not be content with the fare which I give to myself, and that my son [the young John Stuart Mill] whom I destine to be an emulator of all the noblest benefactors to his race, should hereafter be able to boast that he had seen General Miranda. My wife too has heard so much about General Miranda that I can assure you her female curiosity is at no moderate pitch.[87]

On his return to Venezuela Miranda carried with him the ideas as well as the friendship of Mill and in one form or another these found their way into the intellectual life of the revolution.[88]

One of the most distinguished public figures who listened and learned from Miranda and agreed with many of his proposals, especially his insistence on independence, was the Duke of Wellington, still, in Miranda's time, Sir Arthur Wellesley. In 1808 Wellesley supported the idea of an expedition to Spanish America and consulted closely with Miranda in its preparation. When it was aborted, no one in the government dared break the news to Miranda and the unenviable task fell to Wellesley himself. Writing later, in the 1830s, Wellington recalled his meeting with Miranda on 9 June 1808: the episode is well known and quoted in Robertson, but it is worth repeating.

> I think I never had a more difficult business than when the Government bade me tell Miranda that we would have nothing to do with his plan. I thought it best to walk out in the streets with him and tell him there, to prevent his bursting out. But even there he was so loud and angry, that I told him I would walk on first a little that we might not attract the notice of everybody passing.

87 Mill to Miranda, 7 May 1809, *Archivo Miranda*, vol. XXII, pp. 344–5.

88 Rodríguez, '*William Burke*' *and Francisco de Miranda*, pp. 343, 509–10, 519–29.

> When I joined him again he was cooler. He said: 'You are going over into Spain … you will be lost — nothing can save you; that, however, is your affair; but what grieves me is that there never was such an opportunity thrown away!'[89]

By the next day Miranda had recovered enough to wish Sir Arthur 'every sort of prosperity and success'.[90] The two remained on good terms. Wellesley continued to see Miranda and whenever he returned from the peninsula he consulted him for news and advice on the Hispanic world.

Four years later Miranda made a last bid for a British alliance. In June 1812, announcing to Castlereagh his appointment as Generalissimo of Venezuela with full powers to treat with foreign states, he expressed his desire for a close and intimate relationship with Britain and his wish to form an indissoluble union between both countries.[91] It was a forlorn request and too late to save Miranda from defeat in Venezuela and death in a Spanish prison.

89 Roberston, *Life of Miranda*, vol. II, p. 23.

90 Miranda to Wellesley, 10 June 1808, *Archivo Miranda*, vol. XVI, p. 184.

91 Miranda to Castlereagh, 2 June 1812, Molini (the bearer) to Hamilton, 4 September 1812, NA, FO 72/171.

3

Miranda and Music

Edgardo Mondolfi Gudat

> You, Captain Miranda, never come to the sacrament of the holy mass. You prefer to stay and play the flute. The flute is a perverse instrument, Captain Miranda. It is said that Flauro, the first general of hell, plays it wonderfully. Flauro, flautist: there must be something in the phonetic proximity.
>
> Danzil Romero, *La tragedia de Generalísimo.*

On 8 July 1785 a salvo of applause ruptured the London night when one of the most numerous and renowned orchestras of the day — the Westminster Abbey Orchestra — played the final chords of the greatest homage George Friederic Handel would ever receive from his chosen country. It was the German master's centennial. Indeed, he had made England his home, and in the end his music was more attuned to the spirit of Protestant England than any other European nation, particularly his oratorios and especially the Messiah. As the eighteenth century ended, Handel continued to enjoy the privilege of being one of the most important presences in the island nation's musical tradition, while many of his fellow composers of the already distant Baroque Age were no longer much in evidence. They had been displaced by the overweening deliriums of Neoclassicism. That is why England set out to celebrate, as never before, that emblematic centenary — with the good offices of several hundred singers and musicians from Westminster Abbey.

Among those present at this explosive sequence of voices and trumpets by Handel was the Venezuelan Francisco de Miranda, then on his first visit to London, where he had arrived in January of that year. London, perhaps then more than at present, was seen in the eyes of the traveller as an extension of the great river that winds its way through it. For his part, Miranda had sailed up to the world's political capital aboard the *Neptune*, to encounter the friends who would play such important roles in the great undertaking his imagination secretly fostered: the revolt of the Spanish American colonies. He also came to London with the express intention of continuing the long pilgrimage. Miranda had started his journey in the United States two years previously, and he now wanted to extend it to the farthest reaches of Europe, completing, in Mariano Picón Salas's happy phrase, the 'cosmopolitan training of his self'.[1] Miranda was at the time 35 years old.

In the orchestra pit that night playing Handel were Pietro Grassi Florio and Richard Potter.[2] They were not only among the best flautists of the time but they would also develop the instrument technically, in that period of rich inventions and structural revolution in music. No doubt Miranda followed closely, through the massed sound, these consummate masters' executions on the transverse flute. After all, this was the instrument that the young colonel from Caracas, now on the run, had learned to play while enduring the silence and enforced leisure of long journeys and other travails of his unloved military career. Miranda had been in the service of Spain, and between 1771 and 1783 had been stationed in North Africa, Cuba, Florida, Jamaica, the Bahamas and Spain itself.

To come to our own particular concern: for how long had Miranda been interested in music and in particular the flute? Unfortunately, the answer is obscure. That is, for example, the opinion of musicologist Alberto Calzavara. He speculated that a man who, from his base in Caracas — 'a city he lived in … until he was twenty-one years of age'[3] — built a library of 6,000 volumes, travelled extensively and learned very much indeed about art in all its forms, may well have played a musical

1 Mariano Picón Salas, *Miranda*. Prologue by Edgardo Mondolfi (Caracas, 1997), p. 52.

2 It is worth remembering that in the eighteenth century the transverse flute replaced the recorder, acquiring its leading role in symphonie orchestras.

3 Alberto Calzavara, *Historia de la música en Venezuela. Período hispano con referendums al tea-room y la danza* (Caracas, 1986), p. 122.

instrument. Yet there is no precise way of proving it. There is, however, the possibility of learning from his biographers about the rudiments of the education he received in Caracas in the 1760s and '70s. And quite possibly one of his teachers, Don Narciso Yépez or Father Santaella, may have shown the value of music at the same time as he took his first steps in Latin. Miranda's biographer José Nucete Sardi noted that Miranda not only attended preparatory classes at the prestigious Academia de Santa Rosa but in 1764 entered the Real y Pontificia Universidad de Caracas, where he matriculated in the Arts Course under don Francisco José de Urbina.[4] It is thus plausible that at either (or both) of these institutions an early inclination toward music may have been awakened.

Beyond that, it is important to remember José Antonio Calcano's opinion that the inhabitants of Caracas became increasingly interested in music during the years that coincided with Miranda's childhood and youth. The Cathedral in Caracas was located just a few blocks from the Miranda family home. As Maestro Calcano affirms, its music, which previously had been such a traditional feature of the colonial town, was then suffering a period of unmistakable decadence. But by then there was quite a lot of music performed outside of the ecclesiastical sphere, as evidenced by the creation of a full orchestra in Caracas between 1750 and 1760. This was a local, *caraqueño* orchestra. Beethoven had not yet been born, Mozart was ten years old; besides some Haydn, what is most probable is that they played Italian compositions, for this was the music predominant in Spain from the beginning of the century.[5]

Calcano also gives credence to the thesis of Miranda's early musical education in Caracas, based on a very revealing fact that Miranda himself recorded in his travel journal when arriving in Spain for the first time in 1771. Miranda, after visiting the Royal Palace in Madrid, noted that he observed a clock, made in Geneva, playing a minuet. After this, a 'Madama' sang the same tune, another played it on the clavichord and finally a shepherd sitting under a tree played the minuet on his flute, without omitting the little finger and head movements that are usual when

4 José Nucete Sardi, *Aventura y tragedia de don Francisco de Miranda* (Caracas, fourth edition, 1956), p. 12

5 José Antonio Calcaño, *La ciudad y su música. Crónica musical de Caracas* (Caracas, 1985), p. 50.

playing this instrument.[6] It was Miranda's noticing that the 'mechanical shepherd' imitated the head movements that are usual when playing the flute that led Calcano to conclude that it was entirely possible that Miranda had learned to play the flute in Caracas. A flautist does have to pull his head back to take air, but this is a fact that someone who has not played the instrument would probably not notice especially.[7]

Without the rigour that musicology requires, and making good use of poetic license, the Venezuelan writer Denzil Romero re-created in a passage of his novel, *La tragedia de Generalísimo*, an auspicious return in Madrid to the flute of his childhood in Caracas:

> A few steps farther, in another store, this one of music instruments, you purchase a boxwood flute with ivory arches and mouthpiece, manufactured in Mons by the renowned artisan Nicolas Marcel Raingo; you always had a special fondness for this instrument; in your Caracas boyhood you learned to play it; yours then was a rustic wooden flute, straight, with no keys or levers, but with a smooth brilliant sound, a flute from which you could obtain, without much strain, different octaves with their own nuances, from the lowest (like a cracked woman's voice) up to the highest, like bird trills persuading children and dolls to dance.[8]

What is certain is that the first solid evidence of Miranda's appreciation of and interest in music does date from the time when he arrived in Madrid to complete his 'imperfect education'. In support of this idea, Professor Miguel Castillo Didier, who has the merit of being, along with Alberto Calzavara, one of the first to examine this aspect of Miranda's life, notes that among expenses listed in his diary for September 1771 there are gifts sent to his family in Caracas including, among other items, 'some sheet music to send home'. On the same date Miranda

6 Francisco de Miranda, *Archivo del General Miranda*, edited by Don Vicente Dávila (Caracas, 1929), Tomo I, *Viajes*, p. 44. The spelling in this and other passages quoted from the *Archivo* has been modernised to make them more accessible to the reader.

7 Calcaño, *La ciudad y su música*, p. 111.

8 Denzil Romero, *La tragedia del Generalísimo* (Caracas, 1983), p. 39.

noted that from the 120 pesos set aside for his expenses he had purchased 'a flute for 9 doubloons'.[9]

Thus it is easy to see that, while all reference to his musical education in Caracas is vague and inexact, when he first arrived in Europe in 1771 his interest in playing and learning about music are beyond doubt. The entire world began to flow through the soul of this Venezuelan when he entered Spain through Cadiz (ironically also the city where he would be imprisoned and die in 1816).

An interesting document is preserved in the Miranda Archive, dating from the time of his passage through Cadiz. This is the 'Instruction for the Conservation of the Transverse Flute', a handwritten and unsigned text on how to use, manage and preserve the instrument. Despite its relative length, it is worth quoting this simple and practical method, found among Miranda's papers:

> Whenever one finishes using this instrument it will be taken apart and cleaned inside with a fine cloth and a cane rod, at least around the mouthpiece, and also the next pieces, and if all of it, so much the better. Afterwards it will be placed in its bag to protect it from the strong impression of the air.
>
> When one wants to use it and has not played it for some days, it will be convenient to rub a little oil into its inner face because the humidity of saliva could affect the wood and split it. Oil must never be rubbed on the outside, and only on the inner part of the holes.
>
> When after some time one notes that the flute has generated tar inside it, take out the stopper and gently scuff the area with a section of cane, making sure that this blunt end does not increase the diameter of said instrument; again setting the stopper in its same place precisely, for any variation would make the entire instrument dissonant. Before replacing the stopper clean all the flute's interior with a cloth to make it perfectly clean, then oil it and note that before applying the oil you must always clean the flute inside with the cloth to dry off any moisture.

9 Miguel Castillo Didier, 'El Precursor Francisco de Miranda y la música,' in *Revista Musical de Venezuela*, año 5, nos. 12–14, January–December 1984, pp. 101–2.

> If the climate is of dry and strong air, redouble your care and apply oil much more frequently to keep the wood fresh and prevent splitting.[10]

For the gallant gentleman the young 'Indiano' aspired to become, the flute was no doubt the perfect instrument. On the one hand it was considered the perfect adjunct to the eighteenth-century grandee, as innumerable portraits of the time attest; on the other, it enjoyed the appreciable advantage of being at once practical, portable and resistant, and was thus very convenient for people who travelled a lot. The third advantage was that, like the trumpet, this was one of the wind instruments with the most promising development at the time, as proved in the latter part of the eighteenth century by the flute's evolution at the hands of masters Potter and Florio. This leads to another question: what type of flute did Miranda purchase in Madrid in 1771?

When Miranda returned from Spain to Havana to serve as captain of the Aragon Regiment, he made a list of his belongings. Thus we know that he possessed at that time two flutes, one of boxwood and another of ebony, both made by Banetti, at a cost of 850 reales the first and 1,000 the second.

In any case, no matter how stylish Miranda wished to be with his flute playing, we are forced to admit that he was never more than an amateur who did not trouble to make the effort required to become an expert player. Both flutes belong to the baroque period, and had a single tone. We infer this from the method found among his papers in Havana, the well known 'Méthode pour apprendre en peu de temps à jouer de la Flûte Traversière, à l'usage de commençants et des personnes plus avancées' (written by the French writer Antoine Mahaut).

An important German author had this to say about the Method: 'Antoine Mahaut's method was published in 1759, soon after the author was obliged to seek refuge in a monastery after escaping from Amsterdam to Paris, fleeing his creditors. The Method is essentially the best record we conserve about common practices in the first part of the eighteenth century.'[11] A review of General Miranda's Archive

10 'Instrucción para la conservación de la flauta travesera,' Archivo del General Miranda (original), Tomo IV, *Viajes*, folios 284–5.

11 Johann George Tromlitz, *The Keyed Flute*, translated and edited with an introduction by Ardal Powell (Oxford, 1996), pp. 31–2.

makes it possible to ascertain that the future Generalissimo had kept only some of the lessons of this Method,[12] possibly keeping these by his side because they were his favourites. As an examination of his Havana belongings (dating from 1782) shows, Miranda already possessed at that period, just after returning from Spain, a respectable collection of sheet music. Among the more important composers, we find Stabinger, Groneman, Filtsz and Richter (of the renowned Mannheim School), the Englishman Wendling, Mozart's favourite flautist, and the Italians Giuseppe Sammartini and Alessio Prati, along with the Spaniards Luis Misón and Manuel Plá and the Frenchmen Laveux, François Martin and De Lusse. This music includes sonatas and solos for flute as well as duos, trios, quartets, quintets, minuets and marches. Miranda's belongings in 1782 also listed a pianoforte, made in England — a new invention, as he remarked. This instrument was of elegant construction and exquisite woodwork.

By June 1783, when Miranda declared himself a deserter from the Spanish Army, he abandoned his captain's stripes to the star-lit Caribbean night and resolved to flee to the United States, carefully concealed in the hold of a vessel sailing from Havana. The very first entry in his *Diario de Viajes* (Travel Diary) recorded this event.[13] As for music, it was very much on his mind during his stay in the United States between June 1783 and December 1784: in Beaufort, North Carolina, he remarked, it was enough to play a little on the flute to conjure the steamy climate, especially the flies and heat.[14] And possibly the most amusing passage of his diary refers to an incident involving music:

> Here's a little anecdote that happened to me here, showing that all the nations of the earth, and even the most civilised, have preoccupations that carry the crassest superstition. One of the days that I spent in this place fell on a Sunday, and being at home and unable to take a walk because of the heavy rain, I took the flute and began to amuse myself playing a piece, upon which the land-

12 Archivo del General Miranda (original), Tomo XXV, *Viajes*, folio 271.

13 Miranda sorted his papers into three sections: *Viajes* (1764–93); *Revolución Francesa* (1792–1808); and *Negociaciones* (1770–1810), which constitute a total of 63 original volumes, organised and bound by himself, and which are in the Academia Nacional de la Historia in Caracas.

14 Miranda, *Archivo del General Miranda* (Dávila ed.), Tomo I, *Viajes*, p. 199.

> lord and the lady of the house, surprised and scandalised, ran off looking for Mr Tocker so that he would intercede with me and stop me from playing the flute and not play on Sunday. Mr Tocker came to me right away and reported this to me; I burst out laughing and of course stopped playing the instrument, with which circumstance the entire family quietened down, and I was obliged to offer an apology for my thoughtlessness.
>
> The same happened in Newberne, when I absentmindedly set to playing cards on a Sunday, and had not a little to do to give satisfaction to those persons and recover my good name, which otherwise would have been irrevocably lost.[15]

Miranda was in the habit of noting in his diary quite severe and disdainful judgements on fanaticism in all its forms, wherever he encountered it. So it was that in Philadelphia in November of 1783 he complained bitterly of the lack of theatres, this kind of entertainment being anathema to Quakers, who were then predominant, although all kinds of other religions and sects were of course permitted there.[16] There were exceptions, to be sure, because he observed that in the house of a prominent Quaker family, the Penns, a private concert was held once a week, with the best musicians present in the town performing. The room was small, and so were, by necessity, both ensembles and audiences. He added: 'This was all the entertainment to be had in Philadelphia during my stay there, which indicates sufficiently that the inhabitants love and cultivate Society, and dancing is the favourite diversion.'[17]

From this period of residence in the United States dates also his habit of copying into his diary the best remarks he heard about the concerts and musical evenings he attended. For example, staying in another part of Pennsylvania where entertainment also consisted solely of ballroom dancing and musical soirées, Miranda noted:

> Bentley's concert, as it is called, is once a fortnight, and the room where it is held is not badly decorated. Among the players Brown's flute stands out; it is of medium merit. The German

15 *Ibid.*, p. 204.
16 *Ibid.*, p. 229.
17 *Ibid.*, p. 272.

> Concert is executed in the same room once a fortnight, alternating with the preceding one. The players are nearly the same ones, so there is little difference. The price of a ticket is 10 shillings, a very high price for the country, so not many people go.[18]

Later, in Boston in August of 1784, Miranda evaluated New England's choral music, noting in his diary:

> Sunday, and in consequence day of the Church … The girls … sang their psalms and antiphonies very well. The method is that a music master instructs all the young ladies of his household and the young men too, and then each one takes his book to church, they separate into three choirs in the upper gallery, and with the direction of the said master, who acts as choir-master, they sing the music, in tune and rather well, though without an organ or any other accompanying instrument. The music's composition and also the singing are the most solemn and ecclesiastical that I have heard until now in this continent.[19]

Later, on 5 September 1784, he noted that he attended a religious service at the Anglican Church in Newport, where psalms were sung with an organ accompaniment. Two days later he spent a day with a family of sober and simple manners where the mistress of the house played the clavichord and sang some little French airs well.[20]

From Boston, after spending 18 months in the United States, Miranda sailed for London, where we find him in June 1785 at the concert celebrating Handel's centennial.

The Venezuelan, however, wanted to travel on, and soon he convinced his friend William S. Smith to accompany him on a tour of the continent's courts and places of interest. Smith was an American colonel, son-in-law and secretary of future President John Adams, at the time still US minister in London. In fact, as his diary records, his first aim was to observe the Prussian army's manoeuvres — under the ancient Emperor Frederick II — considered the best by the military thinkers of the day. Subsequently, because wherever he went he was well received and entertained, Miranda's journey was unexpectedly extended a number of times.

18 *Ibid.*, p. 301.
19 *Ibid.*, p. 272.
20 *Ibid.*, p. 301.

It might be useful to pause here and consider what that European Grand Tour signified in the education of Miranda's spirit, especially in comparison to his Spanish American contemporaries. One of Miranda's best biographers, the American William Spence Robertson, summed up his admiration for that journey in these words:

> No matter how extraordinary Miranda's journey through the United States may have been for a man of his background and time, his tour of the European continent was far more sensational. He was probably the first well-informed native from Spanish or Portuguese America to travel through Europe. Besides contemplating many monuments to the glory of Greece and the grandeur of Rome, he improved his knowledge of certain languages and increased his understanding of military science. He 'inspected the pages of tyranny in the great book of the European nations.' His mind recorded fascinating anecdotes, incidents at royal courts and military camps. Besides the large number of books and pamphlets about Europe he collected, he wrote a diary about his colourful adventures which contains not only a veritable mine of information about the continent's situation but also revelations concerning his secret ambitions.[21]

Certain pages of the diary, the author adds with as much embarrassment as exaggeration, are not suitable for publication. In his opinion, neither the place nor good taste make it possible to do more than allude to certain orgies in which Miranda indulged.[22]

Armed with a letter of credit issued by his new friends in London and in the company of Colonel Smith, Miranda entered the Continent by way of Rotterdam. A singular and passing strange country, is how he described Holland. He went to Haarlem first, where he was struck by the cathedral's famous organ. 'The church of this city', he noted, 'is renowned for its organ, built in 1738 by a local man named Christian Muller, and consisting of 8,000 pipes … We entered the church with the expectation of hearing it played, but the musician was so arrogant that we decided to let go the idea.'[23]

21 William Spence Robertson, *La vida de Miranda*, translated by Julio E. Payró. Second edition revised and compiled by Pedro Grases (Caracas, 1982), p. 73.

22 *Ibid.*

23 Miranda, *Archivo del General Miranda* (Dávila ed.), Tomo I, *Viajes*, p. 358.

In any case, Frederick the Great of Prussia's military exercises were the journey's main purpose, thus Miranda and Smith went on to Potsdam, where they experienced for the first time the disconcertingly hospitable nature of the tough Prussians. There Miranda observed every last detail of the Palace of Sans Souci — the old monarch's place of retirement — before continuing to Berlin, the true capital of his dominions. The Venezuelan and the American did in fact witness several of the more famous reviews of gendarmes and hussars. Miranda was critical of Frederick II's absolutism and despotic nature, but he was all admiration at the king's yearly expenditure of 100,000 crowns on the Italian theatre.

Though he glimpsed the monarch in several rooms at the palace, Miranda did not have the opportunity to discover that behind Frederick's eternal irritation — probably the result of his gout — there lurked the fine spirit of a notable flautist, though he no longer played. In fact, the composer J.J. Quantz had written an extraordinary amount of flute music for the king. It is possible that by the time Miranda met him the old man was no longer charmed by jubilant music. In fact, Frederick the Great was to die just a year later, the victim of longstanding bad health.

In Prague, his next stop, Miranda again showed an interest in organ music. There he met Franz Josef Oehlschlägel, a prolific Bohemian composer of church music, and also a monk, choirmaster and organ-builder (known also by his monastic name Jan Lohelius). He had spent 30 years building the great organ at Strahov Monastery in Bohemia, and he politely satisfied Miranda's curiosity, drawing a powerful bellow from the unique instrument. Mozart improvised on the organ when he visited Strahov in 1787.

The travellers' next stop was Vienna, in the eighteenth century the city where Italian, Bohemian and German musicians went for Imperial patronage. The Austrian capital, with its court, theatres, wealth and aristocratic patrons, as an important critic tells us,[24] impressed Miranda right away. With Colonel Smith he went to the National Opera, where he saw Emperor Joseph II and his brother Maximilian, often seen there. In his diary, Miranda listed the best singers of the day, among whom were Joseph Adamberger (for whom Mozart created the role of Belmonte in the *The Abduction from the Seraglio*), Francesco Benucci (a

24 Arthur Jacobs, *Breve historia de la música occidental* (Caracas, 1991), p. 175.

buffo bass specialised in the operas of Mozart and Salieri who would later be the first Figaro) and the English soprano Nancy Storace (famous because Mozart composed a cantata for her).

By October of that year Miranda had set his sights on the vast eastern reaches of the empire, stretching to the end of present-day Hungary. But in Vienna Colonel Smith decided to separate, leaving Miranda to go on alone in his quest for knowledge and experience. The Venezuelan then travelled to Ensitel and Esterháza Palace, which turned out to be the high point of his European journey — at least in musical matters. Franz Joseph Haydn lived out his very quiet life there, a life so lacking in personal incidents or worldly disturbances that — as one critic put it — had he not been an artistic genius of the first order, the outside world would never even have known he existed.[25]

In that isolated Esterházy dominion, Haydn served as musical director under the benevolent but authoritarian regime of his protector, Prince Nicholas. Miranda's visit was special — as musicologist Robert Stevenson remarked — because it was Haydn's first contact with the Latin American world.[26] Haydn's most important twentieth-century biographer, H.C. Robbins Landon, concurs, noting that this visit pleased the composer.[27]

After the imperial family itself, in the Habsburg orbit the Esterházy family was considered the highest-placed, wealthy enough to have built in their family seat of Esterháza, a palace with 120 bedrooms, considered by many travellers of the time to be like a second Versailles.

Beyond being composer-in-residence, Haydn also served as musical director for the vast Esterházy entertainment machine. Nevertheless, he managed to write most of his operas and major orchestral works and chamber music there between 1766 and 1790. A Haydn specialist notes that members of the royal family and the aristocracy frequently visited the palace and that music was one of the principal entertainments offered there. Prince Nicholas was proud of his corps of musicians and wanted it to be considered the best in Europe.[28]

25 James Cuthbert Hadden, *Haydn* (Buenos Aires, 1944), p. 71.

26 Robert Stevenson, 'Los contactos de Haydn con el Mundo Ibérico,' in *Revista Musical Chilena*, año XXXVI, January–June 1982, no. 157, p. 19.

27 H.C. Robbins Landon, *Haydn Chronicle and Works; Haydn at Eszterháza, 1766–1790* (London, 1978), p. 673.

28 Hadden, *Haydn*, p. 77.

Miranda noted in his diary that he had letters of introduction for Haydn and that the composer immediately had him take the grand tour of the palace and its environs, and appreciate the rococo architecture. In Miranda's words:

> The famous Haydn, for whom I brought letters, accompanied me immediately and showed me the entire Palace, the Library, the Painting Gallery, the Cascades, the Theatre, etc. The theatre, in use the year round, costs [Prince Nicholas Esterhazy] 30,000 florins a year and the salaries are paid in perpetuity. In the evening I went to the opera, saw the prince there with his niece and his mistress, a vulgar woman. He might be around seventy. The performance was cold. The orchestra, twenty-four instruments. Haydn played the clavichord.[29]

The following day Miranda visited the spacious gardens with Haydn — in a carriage offered to him by Nicholas in person — admiring the grottos, hothouses, hermitages and temples. He noted artlessly: 'I spoke a lot about music with Haydn and he agreed with me about Boccherini's merit.'[30]

Wherever Miranda travelled in Europe, the rich musical culture had something to offer him. Italy, where his tour took him next, was justly famous for its great musical tradition. Miranda disembarked in Trieste, where, as he recorded in his diary, he went to hear the young violinist Carl Cannabich play. This musician's own compositions belong to the third generation of the renowned Mannheim School. After this, learning that there was no ship sailing for his intended destination, Asia Minor, Miranda decided to spend some time in Italy.[31] From Trieste he went on to Venice, where the startling beauty of the city of the Doges moved him deeply. He recorded in his diary a meeting with a group of Jesuits who had been expelled from Spain and the New World, and contributed to his ideas about emancipation. But among them too was Abbot Esteban de Arteaga, the author of an essay on the opera, well known in its day, the *Rivoluzioni del Teatro Musicale Italiano*; Miranda noted that he had liked the book. In the company of the opera-loving Jesuit, our traveller went to a spectacle near St Mark's. Unfortunately the occasion was marred by buffoonery and

29 Miranda, *Archivo del General Miranda* (Dávila ed.), Tomo I, *Viajes*, p. 435.

30 *Ibid.*

31 Robertson, *La vida de Miranda*, p. 57.

indecency, which were made bearable only by his new friend's musical erudition.[32] A few days later Miranda embarked for Verona. There he saw the famous castrato soprano Gasparo Pacchiarotti. Stendhal wrote that at a performance of Ferdinando Bertoni's Arterase, at one point Pacchiarotti's singing was such that, in mid-aria, the musicians were moved to gradually cease playing. Pacchiarotti approached the orchestra pit enquiringly, only to find the maestro barely able to mouth, 'I am in tears, sir'.[33] This castrato, whose voice competed with the brilliance of trumpets, was once summoned to the private apartments of Marie-Antoinette for a private performance. For his part, Miranda wrote: 'Pacchiarotti, whose expression, manner and grace in singing exceed anything I have seen or imagined … does despite this mumble and sing false notes.'[34]

After Verona came Bologna, Mantua, Parma and Modena where, describing the Ducal Palace's library, Miranda observed: 'One also sees certain modern musical instruments, among them a viola and a violin, very beautifully formed.'[35]

On 25 January 1786 Miranda reached Rome. His diary abounds in observations of the city's ancient and modern buildings; he also took notes on a number of highlights: Michelangelo's Moses, a mass heard in the Sistine Chapel and a concert he attended in the company of a Cavaliere de la Planargia. He complained that they could not sit together — it was too crowded — but '… we chatted and drank our sorbets. An opera where only the first buffo, Bruni, had any merit, that exhausted us until 11 with its damn (sic) ballerinas in black trousers.'[36]

A little later he journeyed farther south, and noted that while elsewhere gentlemen spent their money on horses and servants only, the city of Naples owed its advanced state to music and those who enthusiastically contributed to it. He applauded the many young students learning at the Conservatory and remarked that castrati were fully supported and 'they are marvellously maintained', adding 'something good had to come from such an ordeal'.[37]

32 Miranda, *Archivo del General Miranda* (Dávila ed.), Tomo II, *Viajes*, p. 13.

33 Patrick Barbier, *Historia de los castrati* (Buenos Aires, 1990), p. 101.

34 Miranda, *Archivo del General Miranda* (Dávila ed.), Tomo II, *Viajes*, p. 27.

35 *Ibid.*, p. 35.

36 *Ibid.*, p. 64.

37 *Ibid.*, p. 103.

In Greece, the next stop on the European pilgrimage, music also found its way onto the pages of his diary. Disembarking in Piraeus, he was immediately struck by the clear echoes of paganism echoing in the country's melodies. The Greeks seemed untiring in their love for song, music and laughter. The traveller from the Tropics noted: 'How given to music is this nation! Everybody sings.'[38]

Soon after arriving in Athens, he was given the unusual opportunity of witnessing a young Greek's conversion to Islam. He noted that the music was entirely Turkish and then went on to describe the musicians' principal instruments: 'Drums much larger than ours, played with a single stick, and a kind of smaller clarinet, with a higher sound; both instruments seemed better suited to playing military music than ours.'[39] In Smyrna, where he tried in vain to see the ruins of Troy through a spyglass, Miranda again remarked that the Greeks sang continually and that for them 'there appeared to be no amusement without music'.[40] A few leagues on, the travelling *caraqueño* arrived in Scutari, a suburb of Istanbul, and did not fail to note this detail: whether or not Islam permitted it, the country's musicians were happy to have the occasional drink of wine, as Miranda noticed when watching a group of musicians playing under a tree. They played Turkish music with four or five instruments: a viola d'amore, small flutes and a lyre, just as described in antiquity.[41]

With the passport the Austrian minister in Constantinople offered him, Miranda set out for Russia in September of 1786 on a ship sailing along the coast of the Black Sea. He was probably the first Venezuelan (and the first Latin American) to travel that route, over the Crimea to Kiev. There he temporarily joined Tsarina Catherine II's court.

Before reaching the Crimea, however, Miranda had been obliged to suffer quarantine in the Kherson, such periods of enforced isolation being a hazard of travel at the time. The Venezuelan's journey was thus delayed in this fashion. Even so, the regime when so confined did permit him some entertainment that included a little music. Like any other place, the Kherson quarantine facility had its own way of creating and

38 *Ibid.*, p. 122.
39 *Ibid.*, p. 128.
40 *Ibid.*, p. 135.
41 *Ibid.*, p. 161.

enjoying music. 'I asked a colonel', related Miranda, 'what he did to train these musicians who played all music passably, and on all sorts of instruments. And he answered that with no more master or agency than the usual one for Russian regiments: the stick. The fact of the matter is that every man learns with no more master or agency than the stick, that if he does not learn and do as he is told, the stick soon falls on his ribs. It's incredible that this remedy never fails.'[42]

The Russian portion of Miranda's great tour is perhaps the richest one in musical references, as the diary shows. Let us merely note a few examples. First, with Prince Gregory Potemkin, the Russian prime minister and military chief, no less, Miranda heard some Boccherini quartets, actually somewhere near where he had been quarantined in Kherson. With Potemkin, who showed him around the Crimean Peninsula (conquered from the Turks through military action) the traveller saw the interesting spectacle of hunting horns, much liked and used by the Russian nobles. As he noted on 25 January 1787:

> At midday I went to Potemkin's house. We had good company and in the afternoon, the renowned music of the Russian hunting horns, which is really the best thing invented to date to provide a full but also agreeable sound. There were more than 65 musicians and the horns range in size from over 12 feet to the smallest of less than one foot; each horn plays a single note, so several players used two of them. The whole produces an effect like an organ, with the advantage that the horns give a crescendo very nicely, and the diminuendo, with the excellence of a fuller and lovelier sound than any other instrument, even the trill can be played very well with two different horns … We listened to this music for a great part of the evening, and the Prince made them play a great variety of music. I liked best an oratorio of Sarti's; it was created for the occasion and I though it was an excellent composition.[43]

The reference to Sarti is interesting. Soon after Miranda was presented in Kiev to the greatly renowned Tsarina of all Russia (an encounter that has

42 *Ibid.*, pp. 208 and 212.

43 *Ibid.*, p. 247.

given rise to all kind of conjecture about the degree of intimacy granted to the Venezuelan Creole), Miranda met Giuseppe Sarti, who was the director of the Italian Opera in St Petersburg and a friend of Mozart's. Catherine took interest in Sarti's work and was of course quite free in her opinions of his operas and oratorios. Miranda exchanged opinions with the composer on the music of their contemporaries, giving rise to the following passage of his diary: 'The musician Sarti arrived from St Petersburg and we had a long talk about the music and merit of Boccherini and Haydn; he told me that the former was more of a genius while the latter knew more about music. He spoke too of Handel, whose compositions he admires a lot. It seems to me that Sarti is a deep man about the theory of music and composition, which he knows mathematically.'[44]

His sensational adventure then took him from the heart of Russia to the Scandinavian countries, where he inspected asylums, hospitals, mines and gaols. There, his sex life apparently became not only active but also somewhat spicy. At every inn at which he stayed he eyed the feminine complement, and if there was no chance of love, often he did at least manage to engage the maid or the landlady in a flirtation. Of course, they did not all succumb to his charm, and when they did not he referred to them as honest ladies. Beyond that, he sometimes also called 'honest' the women whose bodies he bought, if he observed that poverty was the evident cause of their offer.[45]

Certainly, Scandinavia for Miranda was not all inspections of the harsh reality of prisons or libidinous swoops. He also had time for the company of principal artists and to record in his diary his admiration for the architecture of the main Scandinavian cities. In Sweden the patronage of Gustav III was at its height, benefiting the opera especially. He went to the opening of a piece written for Stockholm's new opera house and noted: 'Here there is a new Opera House, a piece of good architecture, and possibly the best in Europe seen from the outside.'[46] He spent an evening inside it, describing the actual theatre as '... magnificent and elliptical in form', and hearing the notable soprano Sophia Standing, who had just triumphed in Berlin. Our Creole traveller also

44 *Ibid.*

45 Antonio Egea, *Francisco de Miranda* (Madrid, 1987), pp. 72–3.

46 Miranda, *Archivo del General Miranda* (Dávila ed.), Tomo III, *Viajes*, p. 3.

learned that the king spent 80,000 rix a year on the maintenance of the opera. After the show, he shared some roast meat with the singer and then '… had coffee in Mademoiselle's room, which was next door'.[47] A week later, visiting the *prima donna* at home, she graciously sang 'a few things' for him, and he could not but add: '… and very well, too'.[48] In this case, as in others during his passage through these icy parts, his musical sense went hand in hand with his womanising.

In December of that year of 1787, in Fargestad, Denmark, Miranda attended a benefit concert in a theatre the city's Masonic lodge maintained; there was a full house, with a good violin and an agreeable voice, it seems. Most certainly the company was agreeable too, for Miranda sat with the wife of one of his hosts, the tempting Madame Hall. In the event, Miranda thanked Mr Hall for his kindness and equally — and just as politely — warmed Mrs Hall's bed whenever the circumstances permitted. 'Then I went home to write, to go tomorrow with Monsieur and Madame Hall (who has offered to take me to bed if there is a chance) to their country house',[49] was how one of his annotations ended.

His study of all sorts of things led him to conclude that the Danish royal family was irreparably devoured by hereditary defects, making the kingdom ungovernable. And it was in fact at the opera where Miranda saw the afflicted king and confirmed the gossip heard on the street:

> I went to the Comedy … the theatre is somewhat small, and not badly shaped … There was a Danish comedy, which is the only spectacle they put on … The actors were bad, and the orchestra very good and numerous. So that if they had played a concert it would be worth more than the entire spectacle. But what struck me and occupied my attention the whole time was the Danish royal family … The king looks very young, but what a sad spectacle to see him constantly grimacing and moving his eyes, showing plainly that he is not quite sane … at the end of each act he gets up and walks to and fro … He looks at the people around him, speaks to them and they pay no attention. When the show resumes he sits down again, etc …[50]

47 *Ibid.*, p. 31.
48 *Ibid.*, pp. 43–4.
49 *Ibid.*, p. 84.
50 *Ibid.*, p. 106

At the end of his description of so evident signs of mental disorder, Miranda consigned the inevitable piece of wisdom on politics, applicable to so many rulers: 'Oh! What pause a nation whose head is in this state gives us!'[51] The Danish king's grimaces, which he had seen so closely, according to José Nucete Sardi, made a deep impression on our traveller.

After Denmark, Miranda set out for Hamburg, re-entering Germany with some new and very good letters of introduction.[52] In Schleswig he found that the powerful Prince of Hesse was given to splendour and also had some interest in spiritual matters. Possibly Hesse saw in the South American traveller and future hero some measure of generous passion mixed with a very tropical lack of caution for, casting Miranda's horoscope, he concluded that the South American would bring good fortune to many people who had none, and would be remembered. Was Miranda attracted or terrified by this? We do not know. In the event, he thanked the prince and promised to communicate with him, should any of it come true.

In Hamburg Miranda was able to appreciate that the Bach dynasty's merit was still much in evidence. He then left Germany and again passed through Holland (where he had entered the Continent), and then visited Belgium, Strasbourg and the north of Italy, to finally travel up the Rhine Valley to Switzerland. Roads in the region, he noted in his diary, reminded him of the one between Caracas and its seaport La Guaira. In Chesne he noted in his diary that he visited Madame Necker, a relative of Louis XVI's finance minister; it was the autumn of 1788 and the poor king and his head would part company in the not too distant future. As to Madame Necker, fortunately she was 'young and of pleasing appearance'. As to her talent for music, the tourist, severe arbiter of the arts that he was, acknowledged that she had 'some education'. He did have the opportunity to enjoy her singing, in any case.[53]

For a short time, Miranda was able to take refuge in the delicately scaled romance of the Swiss countryside. His diary entries of that time are bucolic and reflective of a contemplative moment. But this did not last, for soon he was on the Riviera, where the enchantments of the

51 *Ibid.*

52 Nucete Sardi, *Aventura y tragedia*, p. 87.

53 Miranda, *Archivo del General Miranda* (Dávila ed.), Tomo IV, *Viajes*, p.43.

night swept him away. France was of course a nation in conflict, with the Revolution about to ignite, but just then Miranda was not concentrating on the political drama. His notes reflect purely artistic and scientific interests; and of course the music critic continued to grind along: in Lyon, 22 November 1788, Miranda wrote:

> When it was about 5:30 in the afternoon, the hour the spectacle commences, I went to the theatre, paying 3 francs for a seat in the stalls. The hall is not bad, with three tiers of loggias and an upper gallery; but the stage is proportionately small. We were given *Orpheus and Eurydice*, Glück's opera, but savaged in a French way. There is not even one fairly good actor, they are all mediocre.[54]

In Montpelier, at the beginning of 1789, the fateful year for the French monarchy, Miranda continued to exercise his critical spirit: 'I went to the theatre, a passable building, with a better-shaped hall than that of Marseille (horseshoe-shaped), smaller; but the decoration in bad taste ... actors and music pretty awful.'[55] We are not certain how long Miranda originally intended his first European journey to be when setting out four years previously, in July of 1785. What is certain is that in the spring of 1789 he still had a few months left in which to enjoy the splendours of France. In Brede he visited the castle where Montesquieu had lived. He also drank chocolate and conversed with the Abbé Raynal, already immobilised by rheumatism, Picón Salas tells us, but still with much to say about the Spanish American situation and especially about the grave days awaiting France.[56] Just as the crucial meeting of the *États Généraux* which would set France on its new historical course loomed on the horizon, Miranda had his final tastes of the French musical world. Two of them deserve mention. In Bordeaux, during the intermission of Glück's *Armida*, he saw the (male) dancer Jean Dauberval perform (in his diary Miranda speaks of 'Madame Doberbál'); this dancer had become notorious after introducing into his dance interpretation elements which the aristocrats considered 'inadequate'. Miranda was thrown into confusion at this revolutionary talent for the dance, for he noted, 'Madame

54 *Ibid.*, p. 99.
55 *Ibid.*, p. 210.
56 Picón Salas, *Miranda*, p. 56.

Doberbál has danced with more taste than I have ever seen in its kind … her foot is large, however.'[57] The other episode concerns a young writer, singer and pianist, Amélie Candeille, who seven years previously had made her debut in the role of Glück's Ifigenia and who would become, twenty-some years later, a furious opponent of Napoleon's from exile. In the pages of his diary devoted to his stay in Aigrefeuille, Miranda took note of Mademoiselle Candeille's talent at a concert where the young woman not only played the pianoforte brilliantly but also demonstrated how acute was her artistic sensitivity:

> Mademoiselle Candeille played excellently. She has a brilliant and clean execution, a delicate touch and tasteful expression. During her second piece a string of her instrument snapped, which muddled the sound a little … She became disturbed … the audience encouraged her and applauded … but she withdrew in tears and near to fainting. With all this, she interested the assembly even more, and came back and played notably, to be sure.[58]

Two days later he noted with irritation,

> I have observed something during these days which is proof of French frivolity and the vertigo of fashion. Because Mademoiselle Candeille played the pianoforte well and the incident was so noticed, the next morning all the fashionable ladies were purchasing pianofortes, and on my walk this morning I saw more than eight being carried out on to the street from the store![59]

In Paris the Venezuelan fell ill with a severe cold and rose only to take the coach for Calais for the Channel crossing. As a precaution, for Miranda was always fleeing the agents of Spain (who were more active and numerous than ever in the France of their Bourbon cousins), he travelled as Monsieur de Meiroff. His passport declared that he was a 'Lithuanian merchant'.

Back in London in July 1789 — and until his death in La Carraca at Cadiz in July 1816 — his interest in music was to decline just as much as his political and military commitments grew. At least that is what his

57 Miranda, *Archivo del General Miranda* (Dávila ed.), Tomo IV, *Viajes*, p. 232.
58 *Ibid.*, p. 255.
59 *Ibid.*, p. 259.

archive shows, for the traces of any interest in music shrink to just a few programmes from the renowned concerts organised in Hanover Square by Johann Peter Salomon, the violinist and future protector of Haydn in London. But this loss of interest in music may be only apparent, for Miranda never again kept immense detailed records like those of his first European tour. This could explain why we have been left with no details of the musical performances he heard and the artists he met — and there must have been many in the musical capital London already was. Even so, among the records, drafts and notes of his extensive archive, there are two curious musical scores from a later time: a version of the Marseillaise published by the French War Department in 1792. This has the merit of being the authentic revolutionary song, without the more martial style that would subsequently characterise the French anthem. This is possibly something Miranda carried with him while serving as an officer with the forces of the French Revolution in Belgium and Holland in 1792 and 1793.[60] The other musical score is linked to the 1806 expedition to the Venezuelan coast; it is a march by Joseph Major, scored for flute and pianoforte. Though any conclusion is speculative, it is possible that Miranda planned to use this music as a basis for the anthem of the new republic.[61]

On ending these pages about Miranda seen principally as amateur flute player, friend of Glück and admirer of Boccherini — music lover — it may be pardonable to return to something more general, quite obvious to us all, but nevertheless notable: Miranda witnessed the two most important revolutions of his time, the American and French Revolutions, and was the promoter of the third, the Hispanic American Revolution. He was also one of the best-travelled Hispanic Americans of his time and had many notable experiences, in Europe especially, and the opportunity to experience briefly its courts, sights and salons. And as Mario Briceño Iragorry noted, in Europe Miranda represented a world struggling to come into its own in the universal order of nations.[62] Obvious or not, one does remain impressed by the calibre of

60 Archivo del General Miranda (original). Tomo XX, *Revolución Francesa*, folio 74.

61 *Ibid.*, Tomo XVII, *Negociaciones*, folio 148.

62 'Sentido y presencia de Miranda,' in Mario Briceño Iragorry, *Discursos académicos y tribuna patria e historia* (Caracas, 1983), p. 117.

the people the Venezuelan met in those long journeys through North America and Europe, including George Washington, Tsarina Catherine the Great and William Pitt the Younger, among politicians, the philosopher Juan Gaspar Lavater, Edward Gibbon and the art critic Antoine Quatremère de Quincy. Miranda became a very cultured and well-travelled man and because of this deserves to be remembered as the most cosmopolitan of Venezuelans.

4

Some Reflections on Miranda as Soldier

Malcolm Deas

My interest in Miranda as soldier originates in a simple curiosity. Was this man, so imposing a figure that he frightened the first soldier of his age, the Duke of Wellington, who with the rank of general held a significant command at Valmy and whose name is on the Arc de Triomphe, any good? Can his ignominious military end be attributed to his luck running out, to incapacity finally exposed? How much of a real soldier was he?

In reading his biographies again, I have drawn other conclusions about this side of his career, about the nature of international military life in his era, about its importance to him, which also seem to me to be worth airing.

The study of Miranda is in some ways too easy: few men have taken such care to document their own lives, and to borrow a phrase, he has 'thrust himself neck and crop between the jaws of time'.[1] The personal archive of Miranda has been available in print for years, and information about him was always abundant: from an early age he left tracks in most of the public archives of Europe, as in his own hemisphere. He has been fortunate in his biographers, even the early ones being still worth reading. There is a consequent danger of taking this vast documentation as an indisputable indication of importance, influence, intelligence, competence, ability … Yet occasionally it crosses the reader's mind that there may be less to the person than the sum of all these many minutely recorded parts. Perhaps, perhaps not.

1 The phrase was applied by Graham Greene to Samuel Butler's aim in keeping his *Notebooks*, which are modest indeed compared with *Colombeia.*

Part of the pleasure of reaching a more considered judgement is to place oneself in the hands of one of Venezuela's finest historians. I have relied on Caracciolo Parra Pérez, particularly on two of his works, *Miranda et la Revolution Française* and *Historia de la Primera República.*[2] Neither of these works has been surpassed: few diplomats can ever have used what it is hardly right to call their leisure to such productive ends as did Parra Pérez, few professional historians are so professional. His patriotic motives do not spoil his judgement, he is respectful, but never uncritical, and every now and again there is even wit. He is a master. Most of my reflections relate to Miranda's earlier career, before the expeditions and his involvement in the First Republic.

The early military career certainly excites curiosity, culminating as it does in the revolutionary command that makes him 'homme de quatre-vingt douze et de quatre-vingt treize', not the only foreigner to be honoured with a statue and an inscription, but a rare honour all the same. How did he come to qualify? How did he become a soldier at all, what was the sum of his previous military experience? How does his French military experience look when examined closely? How many men did he command, what challenges did he meet and how did he acquit himself? How did his contemporaries see him there? Is there anything in his performance that prefigures his later military failure in his native land? Was he — it is too hard to resist the phrase — a chocolate soldier, or something more? Was his French command just another coincidence in a very serendipitous career, an opportunity seized by an opportunist, or something more?

My conclusion is that it was something more, and that Miranda as a soldier does deserve to be taken seriously, both for his genuine military capacity and for what being a professional soldier signified in this era.

Francisco de Miranda was the son of a soldier of sorts, a Canarian officer in one of the militias of Caracas. He therefore came from at least a quasi-military background, and he chose a military career. He spent a decade in the military service of the Spanish crown, and though it was not all spent in operations that commanded the attention of the world, the experience was varied and at times intense enough.

2 C. Parra Pérez, *Miranda et la Révolution Française* (Paris, 1925); *Historia de la Primera República de Venezuela*, 2 vols. (Caracas, 1939).

In 1772, at the age of 22, Miranda was a captain in an infantry regiment. In 1774 he saw action in Algiers, and in 1775 in the defence of Melilla. His record was studious, and a desire to study in Prussia figures in his record; he showed ambition. He was, however, not an altogether easy subordinate. In 1780 he was a captain in the Regiment of Aragon, an aide de camp to General José María Cagigal, serving under him in the siege of Pensacola, in Florida, a formal two-month operation of some magnitude. He rose to the rank of colonel, and in this first decade of his career was at times close to the centre of military affairs that were more important than our Anglo-Saxon view of the times usually credits. This was a genuine military apprenticeship, in which he sometimes earned the admiration of his superiors. As Parra Perez summarises it, 'Il avait fait pendant dix ans la rude apprendisage de la guerre.'[3]

While serving in the Bahamas and Havana he became involved in the complications and conflicts that were to lead him to abandon the Spanish service, and to embark on his long career of itinerant conspiracy and, to use the eighteenth century term, projecting.

As with everything else about Miranda, that is dauntingly well documented. It can be briefly resumed here: he passed from the United States to England, and in 1785 passed to the continent, journeyed to Prussia, Hungary and Italy and thence to Turkey and Russia, to Scandinavia and back to England, before passing again to France and resuming an active military career.[4]

Pursuing our particular line of reflection, how military was this tourism? Miranda did from time to time inspect fortifications, and in Prussia he did, with King Frederick's permission, attend one of those military parades for which Prussia was so justly famous. Nonetheless, military matters do not seem to have been his preferred object of study. Miranda studied everything, including Swedish runes and the court theatre of Drotihgholm, and Danish prisons. He was in that typical of the generation that lived in the light of the Encyclopédie and a person of vast curiosity, and perhaps of *vastes connaissances*, an impression he frequently made and liked to make. One inserts the 'perhaps', because one

3 Parra Pérez, *Miranda et la Révolution Française*, pp. xv–xvi (hereafter cited as *Miranda.*)

4 A one-volume resumé of these travels is provided by Josefina Rodríguez de Alonso, *Le siècle des lumières conté par Francisco de Miranda* (Paris, 1974).

is never quite sure with Miranda about the depth of his knowledge, while one never doubts its width.

What does however strike one forcibly about these travels is the degree to which Miranda's military rank and background gave him the desired entrée in such a range of countries. Before the Revolution it kept him out of France, where he would on Spanish insistence have run the risk of arrest as a traitor to his king's service, but elsewhere it served him very well indeed, and it brings home to one an aspect of eighteenth century life that deserves emphasis in any consideration of his career.

The professional soldier, the holder of a military commission, was a member of a sort of freemasonry. Given the military nature of much early freemasonry, the phrase seems to me the more defensible. Be that as it may, as an officer in the Spanish army Miranda had acquired the manners, the accomplishments and the code of a profession that to the eyes of later more nationalist generations was in his time still strikingly cosmopolitan. Its members were formed in a common culture, one open even to such relatively exotic specimens as this disaffected son of a part-time Caracas militiaman. It was still a widespread practice among officers to take service in foreign armies, a practice that indeed persisted well beyond the wars of the French Revolution and of Napoleon. Prior to that era it would not have excited censure or even comment, within the limits of a code of honour that forbade one taking arms against one's own sovereign. Miranda was invited by Catherine to enter her service. Though he declined, he appears to have taken advantage from time to time of the permission accorded him to wear the Russian uniform. It is interesting that to all such offers of military employment he stipulated that he would not serve against Spain in Europe: '... il limita toujours son hostilité contre l'Espagne aux territoires américains et la seule cause au nom de laquelle il consentait a la combattre, c'était la cause américaine'.[5]

It is not easy to think of another background that would have provided him with equal advantages. Miranda naturally continued to inspect the occasional fortress and to watch the occasional parade — there was not so much else to do, apart from play the flute, in Frederick's Berlin — but what impresses one is the social and political success that he enjoyed, not the military side of his successive receptions. Part of that success was doubtless

5 Parra Pérez, *Miranda*, p. xix.

due to the nervousness the Spanish government showed about his activities, which reminds one of his singularity: he was, after all, the highest-ranking Spanish soldier then conspiring against his sovereign abroad. Nonetheless, his career under this aspect is a proof of a pre-Napoleonic career open to talent in the world of eighteenth-century armies.

Miranda's person had qualities that may have owed something to his military background: he was always carefully dressed, and liked uniforms; he was careful about his teeth, habitually well-shaven, always fit to go out on a visit, slept little, rose early and avoided strong drink. Not all soldiers are like that, but the habits of discipline and the air of decision and distinction he had acquired, and the obviously strong sense of his own worth, do owe something to his soldiering. They enabled him to pass as an aristocrat, and indeed in Russia he let himself be known as *M. le Comte*. When challenged about this he replied in defiant terms that it was the equivalent to the Paris custom of referring to English gentlemen as *milord*, to which no sensible person would object. To his patrons and protectors his favourite gift appears to have been field telescopes from the London instrument maker Ramsden: he gave a pair to Prince Potemkin, and later another pair to General Dumouriez.

Some ten years after leaving the Spanish service Miranda resumed his active military career in the defence of revolutionary France. He did so under circumstances that were more than usually confused, a confusion that does not help evaluating his military qualities, but which does highlight something of their nature. The context, like so much of Miranda himself, was full of ambiguities.

The French forces of 1792 and 1793 were a mixture of professionals and amateurs, of troops of the line and volunteers. There were numerous foreign officers in the service: Caracciolo Parra Pérez, describing the situation in 1792, gives the following incomplete list of the more prominent: the 'incapable German' Luckner, at one point commander in chief; Stengel, an outstanding commander of cavalry from the Palatinate; Miacynski, a Pole; Money, Keating, Sheldon, Linch — all English; Depres-Crassier, Vaudois; Moultson, commander of the French fleet at Antwerp, American; Kilmaine, Irish; Stettenhoffen, Austrian. At one point, the idea was mooted of offering the command to the Duke of Brunswick, the commander of the allied royalist and émigré forces ranged against the Convention!

There was much political interference, no strong established military leadership, many jealousies and dubious loyalties and a high degree of administrative improvisation. The low competence of the French was commonly matched by the similarly low level of competence of their opponents. Neither side had got into its stride. It is against this uncertain background that makes judgement of performance particularly difficult, that Miranda's short French military career has to be seen.

The relations he established in Paris were through the Brissotin or Girondin salons, and here his usual social good fortune accompanied him: chez Mme Roland, chez Vergniaud, chez Valazé, chez Julie Talma, chez 'la poétesse Hélena-Maria Williams', Miranda kept company with 'Brissot, Vergniaud, les Chénier, Cambaceres, Chamfort, Bernardin de Saint-Piere … Barère, … Carnot'.[6] Pétion, Mayor of Paris, was much impressed by him and urged him to consider French service. The essential contact for military employment was made with the then minister of war, Joseph Servan de Gerbey. This is in itself interesting, as Servan was a most intellectual soldier, and regarded as one of the leading military writers of the time. Some years earlier he had published a large innovative treatise *Le Soldat Citoyen*.[7]

It is probable that Miranda, with his pronounced bibliophilia and proclaimed theoretical interest in the art of war, in which as Parra Pérez says 'he passed as a master', knew the book, and its author certainly formed a good opinion of him. It was apparently Servan who finally persuaded him to accept a commission in the French forces: 'Je le sollicitai vivement d'aider la France de ses talents dans un moment ou elle embrassait une aussi belle cause', he was to testify later.[8] On 6 September 1792 Miranda was given his passport and orders to join the Armée du Nord under the command of Dumouriez, where he was to take charge of the left division. He straight away departed for the front, taking an edition of Plutarch as a gift to his chief.

6 *Ibid.*, p. 11.

7 Anon, *Le Soldat Citoyen, ou Vues patriotiques sur la manière la plus avantageuse de pourvoir à la défense du royaume*, Dans le Pays de la Liberté [Neuchatel], 1780.

8 Parra Pérez, *Miranda*, p. 17. Servan followed Miranda's fortunes in the field closely and later wrote in his defence. Another commentator on some of Miranda's actions was Jomini, the most widely read military critic of the era. Parra Pérez complains how most subsequent military historians crib Jomini without acknowledgement.

One should not, however, conclude from this decision to serve a revolutionary government that he was a radically revolutionary soldier. He took some care to negotiate terms, on the grounds that by joining the French he would be sacrificing Russian patronage and prospects, and he was at pains to attempt to explain his decision to his aristocratic friends and contacts in Russia and in England — not yet at war with France — how 'un ancien Castillan soit devenu un sans culotte' and to insist that he had no desire to abandon his plans for the liberty of his homeland, still his chief aim in life. He was no Jacobin. All the same, unsurprisingly, Catherine and her courtiers did not approve.[9]

Such was the background against which one has to view Miranda's decision to serve in the French armies and it helps to explain the spirit with which he served. He was not a volunteer enthusiast, he was a professional and his Girondin friends and patrons who had invited him to serve had high hopes of his professional contribution. Once again in this career that falls on the division of two eras, his revolutionary action had something of an ancien régime quality about it. Though committed to the liberty of France, it is hard to imagine among her defenders a figure less *sans culotte.*

The central chapters of Parra Pérez's work provides us with a minute examination of Miranda's activities from his departure for the army in early September 1792 to his arrest on suspicion of treason and incompetence at the end of March 1793. The chapters are fine examples of dense and meticulous military and political history of a type that few historians now have the patience to undertake, and it is impossible to set out all their arguments and conclusions in a short essay like this. The range of documentation is exhaustive, and Parra Pérez shows himself superior in that respect to a number of the grandees of revolutionary historiography of the time, such as Mathiez and Aulard: the footnotes taking them to task are at times refreshingly tart.[10] It is an altogether convincing defence of Miranda's loyalty and straightforwardness, in an ambience where such qualities were rare, and of his overall competence as a commander. Yet he is by no means blind to Miranda's defects. Certain conclusions emerge clearly enough.

First, Miranda did exercise substantial commands. The numbers under his direct command naturally vary, but at their height appear to have reached 70,000, and were usually around 20,000.

9 *Ibid.*, pp. 18 *et seq.*

10 See, for example, *ibid.* pp. 174–5, n. 8.

In the day-to-day conduct of military business he was systematic and punctilious, and his ten-year apprenticeship and that theoretical knowledge of the business of war which was part of his reputation seem to have stood him in good stead. One gets the impression that he knew what he was about, that he was a true professional.

Miranda also commanded in conjunctures that tested his character, his powers of decision, his sang froid, his military and his political judgement, and he emerged from them with credit.

He was present at Valmy, that battle whose outcome so impressed Goethe, who was a witness on the other side. However, the battle itself does not impress Parra Pérez, who thoroughly debunks the common illusion that it was won by Marseillaise-singing volunteers, most of the troops watching what was essentially an artillery action being infantry of the line under the command of former royalist officers. Here again, the presence of Miranda, unaware of the epoch-marking significance later attributed to the battle, has a certain ironic quality about it.

His role was more important in the siege and occupation of Antwerp, a substantial success in itself. The city surrendered with 140 cannons, 3,000 muskets, 361 sabres, large quantities of ammunition and two Austrian standards.

In his subsequent command over its liberated citizens he was certainly equal to the occasion, both militarily and politically, and showed a commendable combination of firmness and tact. The liberated were naturally ambiguous about their liberators, particularly when these promptly demanded large sums of money to sustain their forces.[11] Here Miranda encounters many of those problems later familiar to the would-be liberator of an unwilling Venezuela: how to raise forced loans, how to soothe local political sensibilities, how to present the benefits of the new order, what to do about paper money, how to get on with the Church.[12]

Altogether, he enjoyed more success than failure, and seems to have owed this to his relatively moderate political character and to the disci-

11 The French invaders, in Parra Pérez's considered view, were in general so rapacious and tyrannical that it is no surprise that on the French retreat after Neerwinden the advancing Austrians were greeted as liberators. Miranda's relative restraint should be seen against that background.

12 In the light of the disastrous experiment with paper money in the first Venezuelan republic, it is interesting to note Miranda's reservations about introducing the *assignat* into Belgium.

pline and order he maintained, both in his proceedings with the inhabitants and in the control of his own subordinates and troops. In loans, he could drive a hard bargain, but he was at least clear and decisive. He was always a strict disciplinarian. Though in his official correspondence he used revolutionary language — he refers to 'la classe ci-devant supérieure', 'ci-devant privilegiés' and to 'la majesté du peuple' — he did not favour the sort of political agitation associated with 'clubistes', and there was nothing revolutionary in his own manner. He got on particularly well with the bishop, once again through a common interest in books: the bishop pressed on him the gift of some Latin and Spanish classics.

Dumouriez was impressed. The capitulation, he wrote to congratulate his friend and subordinate, 'porte en même temps le cachot du philosophe et du républicain'. On other occasions he refers to him as 'le sage Miranda … un des meilleurs officiers geraux de l'armée'; 'homme d'esprit et tres instruit, sachant la guerre par theorie mieux qu'aucun des autres géneraux'. Brissot, at a greater distance, was even more impressed and enthused: 'Il faut incendier les quatre coins de l'Europe: notre salut est là. Dumouriez ne peut nous convenir, je me suis toujours défié de lui. Miranda est le général de la chose: il entend le pouvoir revolutionnaire; il est plein d'esprit, de connaissances.'[13]

This was doubtless both excessive praise and a misreading of Miranda's style and temperament. Miranda was certainly aware of the importance of what he referred to as 'le parti civile, politique et révolutionnaire', but he was for the most part careful to leave that to others.[14] Brissot's praise is nonetheless interesting as evidence of Miranda's real prominence in these months. He attracted the attention of figures of

13 *Ibid.*, pp. 76–7.

14 Parra Pérez nonetheless quotes, with a comment that it is not one of his best productions and that is somewhat out of character, a proclamation *Le général Miranda, commandant en chef les armées de la Belgique, à ses braves frères d'armées*, of 13 February 1793: 'Nos forces navales vont couvrir les mers et faire triompher le pavillon tricolore, tandis que vous, glorieux vainqueurs de Valmy, de Jemappes, de Liège, d'Anvers, de Namur, allez renverser de nouveau les satellites des despotes. Courage, union, discipline, surveillance: vous avez vaincu par ces moyens, vous acheverez votre ouvrage et l'arbre de la liberté, planté de vos mains triomphantes, étendra partout ses rameaux bienfaisants. Allons, enfants de la patrie, un nouveau jour de la gloire est arrivé: que l'hymne sacré retentisse partout et soit le prélude de vos succès!'

the first rank; some wished to give him the command of Ste Domingue, and some voted for his appointment as Ministre de Marine.

It is worth quoting in full Parra Pérez's judgements on Miranda as a commander, both for their content and for their style:

> *[Miranda] était froid et hautain, tenace, inaccessible au découragement, d'une fermeté calculée, souvent troublée pourtant par les éclairs d'une subite colère, sachant à la fois commander et se battre; on lui reproche de n'avoir jamais réussi a provoquer l'enthousiasme qui, seul, conduit le troupier français al'accomplissement de grandes tâches.*

> *l'éxuberance de cet inépuisable charlatan [Dumouriez] contrastait singulièrement avec la circonspection de Miranda, pour lequel il est fort probable qu'officiers et soldats n'eurent guère d'affection. Il se montrera de même au Venezuela lorsque, en 1812, il sera nommé généralissime des forces patriotes: il censurera âprement l'indiscipline du troupier, l'inexpérience des officiers, les défaillances d'une administration rudimentaire, blessant ainsi inutilement l'amour-propre de ses subordonnés et décourageant peut-être les meillleures volontés. Entouré d'étrangers, qu'il jugeait seuls capables de bien servir la cause de l'indépendance, ainsi qu'on l'a prétendu, il verra bientôt se tourner contre lui la plupart des patriotes qu'éxasperait son air dédaigneux et le ton cassant qu'il avait adopté. Cet homme s'imposait à l'admiration de tous par sa haute intelligence, sa dignité et la vaste étendue de ses conaissances; mais il ignorait l'art de se faire aimer des subalternes et il méprisait la popularité et la faveur inconstante de la foule. On pourrait dire qu'il vécut toujours enfermé dans la tour d'ivoire de son orgueil; cependant, et ilfaut insister là-dessus, le soldat n'eut jamais à se plaindre de lui. Le témoinage du directeur général des postes de son armée en Belgique, Philippe, est là qui démontre que la légendaire impatience de Miranda ne se manifestait que losque ses ordres étaient mal compris ou mal exécutés: 'Toujours le soldat trouva en lui un abord facile, un intérêt vrai et le désir soutenu de diminuer les plaintes en faisant cesser les besoins.'*

These judgements are based on the minute weighing of the evidence, even the most fragmentary, that is characteristic of Parra Perez's work.

15 Parra Pérez, *Miranda*, pp. 175, 184.

Miranda's command in France and Belgium prefigures so much of the far better known later episodes in the country of his birth, which the author examines with similar patience and critical spirit in his *Historia de la Primera República.* The ambience was of course distinct. In France Miranda commanded for the most part troops of the line, in the company and with the support of experienced professional officers, who whatever their defects knew the basic rules and arts of war. He operated there in the cockpit of Europe, one of the most fought over, mapped, fortified, recruited, foraged, invaded, besieged and defended parts of the world, such a marked contrast with the militarily virtually virgin Captaincy-General of Caracas. Given his character, as displayed in the former field, his failure there was predictable.

Miranda was a soldier of the old regime, an inflexible disciplinarian, short on the arts of military demagogy, unable to adapt himself to the improvisations that the new scene demanded. He was a Coriolanus, a man who did not fawn upon the people — a quality usually attributed to reactionaries rather than revolutionaries, but common enough among them too. His French career shows that he was also personally brave, technically more than competent, concise in his orders, level headed in crisis, dignified and loyal. In short, a true Coriolanus.

5

Love in the Time of Liberation: Francisco de Miranda's Relationships with Women

Karen Racine

The two sexes mutually corrupt and improve each other.
Mary Wollstonecraft, *A Vindication of the Rights of Woman* (1792)

Francisco de Miranda was a man who loved women but who did not need them. He was a soldier, a patriot, a traveller and a schemer. After the fashion of his day, he was also a gentleman and a lover. During his long and eventful life, Miranda had several love affairs and an even greater number of brief sexual encounters. In truth, his loves and his life's work were intimately connected. Not only did Miranda receive financial aid and personal comfort from women at various crucial points in his life, he also viewed them as valuable allies in his romantic quest for universal liberty and happiness. As one whose deepest desire was to free his native continent from the stultifying grip of the Spanish Empire, Miranda was passionately devoted to liberty in all its various manifestations. In the abstract, he respected and admired women's intellectual abilities and wished to see them play a more active role in the public lives of their nations; on a more practical level, he consistently sought out local women and peppered them with questions about their opinions on matters both historical and contemporary. With his favourable opinion of women's political abilities and the necessity of involving them in public life, he was clearly ahead of most of his contemporaries who still viewed women as weak and inferior and preferred to relegate them to the domestic sphere; at the same time, Miranda was not entirely free of more traditional values that required the honour of upper class women in one's family to be protected while allowing unfettered access to the bodies of lesser types of women. In his attitudes to women, just as in all areas of his life, Francisco de Miranda was a man caught between the eighteenth and nineteenth centuries.

Miranda was not a particularly deep or original thinker. Although he claimed to have read widely and his personal library contained hundreds of books in Spanish, French, English, Italian, Greek and Portuguese, essentially Miranda was a soldier and a man of action. His major contribution to Spanish American independence came not in the realm of political theory or philosophy, but rather in his single-minded devotion to the idea that Spanish America should be free and independent. The quixotic Venezuelan general held fast to that dream for nearly 50 years and never stopped peddling his scheme to anyone who would listen. In many cases, his strategy was to convince the wives or sisters or daughters of influential men of the glory and moral righteousness of his vision, and then to employ them as lobbyists in his efforts to persuade their men to support his cause. Women liked Miranda because he liked them.

Francisco de Miranda was born in Caracas in 1750. He was the first child and oldest son of Sebastián de Miranda, a recent immigrant from the Canary Islands, and Francisca Antonia Rodríguez de Espinosa, the beautiful daughter of a local family. Eventually, Francisco was joined by nine other siblings, five of them girls. He does not seem to have been particularly close to his family, however; he left Venezuela in 1771 to enlist in the Spanish army and never saw them again. Indeed, even Miranda's massive personal archive contains few references to his family; there remain a few letters from his sister Rosa and some indication that he knew of both his mother's death in 1777 and his sister Micaela's marriage in 1782, but very little care or concern after that.[1] Miranda followed a typical career path in the Spanish military, serving in garrisons in North Africa from 1774 to 1776 and in Cuba from 1780 to 1783. Facing a court-martial for alleged espionage on behalf of the British, Miranda fled to the United States where he undertook a tour of the country from 1783 to 1784. He sailed across the ocean and then spent

1 Angel Grisanti, *El Precursor Miranda y su familia: primer biografía de la familia Miranda* (Madrid, 1950), p. 263n.

four more years travelling throughout Europe, venturing as far east as Turkey and Russia, where he stayed for a year as the personal guest of Empress Catherine the Great. In 1792, after several failed attempts to persuade William Pitt to support his Spanish American expedition, Miranda enlisted in the armies of the French Revolution and fought for them in Belgium. When the radical Jacobins rose to power, Miranda found himself jailed for two years and eventually returned to England in 1797. Once he finally realised that the British were not going to bankroll his dream, Miranda returned to the United States in 1805 and put together an ill-fated mercenary expedition to Coro in Venezuela in 1806. When that attempt ended in disaster and humiliation, Miranda returned to his young wife and infant child in England and tried to salvage his reputation. His quest received a boost in 1810 when representatives of the new *juntas* [temporary ruling bodies] in Caracas and Buenos Aires sought his aid and counsel in London. At the age of 60, he returned to Caracas and played a key role in the short-lived First Venezuelan Republic. In 1812, after a series of internal revolts and royalist counterattacks, Miranda signed a capitulation with the Spanish general Domingo Monteverde and expected to be permitted to leave the country once again. Instead, he was seized as a traitor to the empire and taken to a Spanish jail in Cadiz where he died frightened and alone in 1816. His life was full of adventures and intrigue, and he enjoyed friendships with many of the era's most important men. He also engaged in significant relationships of varying nature and intensity with women in many countries. His travels and his reading of contemporary thinkers allowed Miranda a unique comparative perspective on the condition of women throughout the Atlantic World.

In his study of banned books in pre-revolutionary France, historian Robert Darnton has rightly pointed out the connection between liberty and libertinism, seeing in the two attitudes 'a combination of free thinking and free living, which challenged religious doctrines as well as sexual mores'.[2] In other words, one's predisposition to challenge authority and to seek freer action in the public sphere also translated into looser attitudes in private behaviour as well. Francisco de Miranda certainly

2 Robert Darnton, *The Forbidden Bestsellers of Pre-Revolutionary France* (New York, 1996), p. 90.

displayed that quality, one so marked among educated gentlemen-philosophers throughout the eighteenth century Atlantic World. Throughout his diaries and personal correspondence there are innumerable instances in which Miranda sought the physical sensation of love without romanticising its significance or exhibiting any braggadocio about the conquest itself. As true adherent of the Enlightenment, Miranda viewed sex as a source of pleasure and as a natural human act, yet it was not his central concern. Although leering biographers have emphasised Miranda's libido and tried to portray him as a Latin lover, the truth is that his behaviour could be downright prudish at times.[3] As an example, Miranda very nearly challenged the Prince of Nassau to a duel in 1786 when the unfortunate man would not stop telling jokes about the loose behaviour of Spanish women.[4]

Miranda had no scruples about treating sex as a business or as an entertaining pastime. Throughout his travels, he often brought women to his bed to alleviate the loneliness of a life spent in wandering exile. For short-term encounters, he seemed to prefer younger and less experienced girls who were sure to submit to his personal charisma and power; for longer-term or emotionally-charged relationships, however, Miranda chose educated, unconventional women with whom he could also enjoy stimulating conversation. There are innumerable references to short-term encounters. In Beaufort, South Carolina, for example, Miranda suggested that the innkeeper's daughters, two teenaged girls deliciously named Comfort and Constance, might continue their conversations with him in his bed.[5] Later on, in Newport, Rhode Island, Miranda discussed various medical cures and scientific discoveries with local celebrity Dr. Newman before the latter suggested a trip to the local brothel as a fitting end to the evening. Ever a devotee of the Greek classics, Miranda euphemistically recorded in his diary that he was

3 Stewart Halpine, *The Altar of Venus: A Biography of Francisco de Miranda* (Bloomington IN, 2000); and Jacques Cazotte, *Miranda 1750–1816: Histoire de un séducteur* (Paris, 2000).

4 Joseph Thorning, *Miranda, World Citizen* (Coral Gables, 1952), p. 49.

5 Francisco de Miranda, *New Democracy: Travels of Francisco de Miranda in the United States 1783–1783*, Judson P. Wood, ed. (Norman, OK, 1963), pp. 10–11. Comfort was 15, Constance was 18.

> led to the temple of one of the best nymphs, where he [Newman] left me well recommended. After he had gone, we directed our steps to the altar and there consummated a solemn sacrifice to Venus. At ten o'clock I returned to my lodging and read until bedtime.[6]

Two days later, the faithful traveller visited his nymph once again to pay joint homage to Venus. Miranda and his companions availed themselves of prostitutes' services throughout their European tour. After a particularly unpleasant journey across Germany, Miranda's travelling companion William Steuben Smith recorded in his diary that he 'bought the cherries of a Brunswick girl — never did any lass dispose of them with more vivacity — she suplied [sic] me during my stay'. So, too, did Miranda. Smith laughed at the memory that 'Miranda had a curious scene with a Virgin to whose questions of conscience he would not for a moment submit'. In all these instances, the sexual experience remained wholly male, something to which the man was entitled and to whom the physical pleasure belonged.

In the late eighteenth century, it seems that prostitution could almost be considered a patriotic duty. King Frederick of Prussia's policies actually protected and promoted that profession, following the opinion of the day that a large population naturally contributed to a powerful nation.[7] The subject of prostitution was much treated by Enlightenment philosophers and salacious novelists alike and, as a man who liked to read about such things, Miranda used his travels to investigate the issue. In order to keep himself warm in the Crimea, Miranda kept his temperature up by sitting near a fire and reading *Le Pornographe*, a serious and popular book by Nicolas Restif de la Bretonne, which recommended the legitimation and regulation of prostitution; Miranda agreed with the philosopher, both on the basis of its potential contribution to public health and for the improved conditions and protection that would be afforded to the women themselves. Restif de la Bretonne also advocated reforms in the areas of education, gender relations, laws and lan-

6 *Ibid.*, p. 134.

7 W.S. Smith, 'Jornal de Prusia, Saxonia, y Austria en el año de 1785,' *Archivo del General Miranda* (Caracas, 1929), vol. I, pp. 393, 414.

guage; he has become known as 'the Rousseau of the gutter'. Once again, liberty and libertinism joined forces in the eighteenth century.

Like others who shared the Enlightenment's rejection of luxury and self-indulgence, Miranda sought to control his own excesses. Once again, this impulse is well recorded. Just as Miranda did not have a favourable impression of either the 'idle and worthless' Venetian nobility, he also tired of wandering from 'bordello to theatre and theatre to bordello'. Similarly, in New London, Miranda was disgusted to learn that a Catalan merchant immigrant named Gabriel Sistaré had taken a mistress despite having a wife back in Spain and that the errant man had had seven children by her; Miranda sniffed that the illegitimate youngsters were 'as wild as their father and as dirty as their mother'. In Holland, he was appalled at what he considered to be the 'incivility' of Dutch women; he was shocked one afternoon to witness one who 'set down her basket and pissed in the middle of the street before the window which I stood at'.[8] When a Greek chieftain sent a harem of dancing girls to entertain Miranda and his party, the Venezuelan was highly offended, declaring their gyrations to be obscene. A Russian female public school teacher was commended for her service to the common good, but as for her appearance, Miranda said she was 'more heavily painted up than a clown'. He also found French women to be vain, ridiculous, frivolous and living in a sort of slavery to fashion. For example, when Madame Candeille made a spectacular musical debut, Miranda observed contemptuously that the next morning he saw no less than eight pianofortes on the street being delivered to jealous ladies who could not bear to be out of the spotlight themselves. From his vantage point, French upper class women's insularity and lack of social concern meant that they were destroying themselves in 'perfectly *mad* fashion, and not doing themselves or anyone else any good by it at all'.[9] After one particularly painful dinner during which he could not manage to engage a single foppish person in a conversation that made any sense, Miranda left in disgust and went back to his room as soon as the meal was finished. In fact, Miranda's negative impressions of women he met

8 Smith, 'Jornal,' *AGM*, vol. I, p. 361.

9 Francisco de Miranda, *Fragments from a XVIIIth Century Diary*, Jordan Herbert Stabler, ed. (Caracas, 1931), p. 168.

during his travels are hard to separate from his growing Spanish American nationalist and republican sentiment. His assessment of these women's faults can be extended in a cartoonish way to indicate the way Miranda characterised their countrymen as a whole.

Miranda's own inclination was to look for meaningful companionship with women and he genuinely felt happy when he thought he saw them escaping their domestic confines and stepping out into new roles. Again, his impressions are often collared by his desire to see the republican experiment in liberty succeed. For example, one of the first things that Miranda thought he noticed upon arriving in the United States in 1783 was the greater freedom of unmarried women to enjoy public space compared to those of Mediterranean Europe or Spanish America. He observed that:

> The married women maintain a monastic seclusion and a submission to their husbands such as I have never seen … Once married, they separate themselves from all intimate friendships and devote themselves completely to the care of home and family. During the first year of marriage they play the role of lovers, the second year of breeders, and thereafter of housekeepers. On the other hand, the unmarried women enjoy complete freedom and take walks alone wherever they want to, without their steps being observed.[10]

Miranda believed that women should be encouraged to attend public gatherings and be welcomed at all places of social intercourse, 'at which the contrast and variety of manners and customs broaden the outlook and create in us an open, frank, and generous manner — a quality sometimes much more valuable in society than those which stem from wealth and vast knowledge'.[11] More outrageously, in 1792 Miranda criticised an all-male French National Convention that was willing to extend civic membership to people of colour but not to women. He wrote to the Girondin Mayor of Paris, Jerôme Pétion,

> To my way of thinking, I recommend just *one thing*, wise legislator: the *women* … Why is it that in a democratic government, fully half of the individuals, the women, are neither directly nor indi-

10 Miranda, *New Democracy*, p. 6.

11 *Ibid.*, p. 56.

> rectly represented although they are subjected to the same severity of the law? Why can they not be consulted at least in the laws that concern them most (marriage, divorce, girls' education, etc)? I must confess that all these things seem to me to be strange oversights and worthy of consideration on the part of our wise legislators.[12]

For all the historical snickering about Miranda's reputation as a slippery Lothario type, it is to his eternal credit that he was one of the very few eighteenth-century men who were able to perceive that liberal ideals logically extended into the realm of something approaching more equal gender relations in the public sphere as well.

Miranda was squarely in the centre of Enlightenment thought when he favoured extending greater (and better) education to women. He enjoyed refined society and conversing with women who were trained in the traditional feminine realms of music and literature; at the same time, he recognised that his adherence to the notion of political liberty had implications for women as well. Following Rousseau's *Emile* and other Enlightenment treatises which uniformly supported improved education for women, Miranda went one step further and advocated political and public roles for them as well. Perhaps because he always felt comfortable in the presence of women, or perhaps because of the novelty itself, Miranda sought out the most interesting and daring women in the cities that he visited. As examples of his pedagogical theories, Miranda held up the persons of Mrs Powell, Miss Sally Shippen, Miss Moore, Miss Molly Coxe, Miss Peggy Chew and 'the Quaker Misses', Susan and Rebecca Morris and Isabella Marshall. His '*amiga querida*' [sweetheart] at the time, Miss Polly Vining, was an exuberant and athletic lass who taught him to skate and to play the popular card game 'Comet'. All these American women combined the new republican ideal of femininity, athleticism and intelligence. He did not even restrict his political talk to women of his own class; in one typical example, when he spotted a female shopkeeper reading Charles Rollin's dense ten-volume work *Ancient History of the Egyptians, Carthaginians, Assyrians, Babylonians, Medes, Persians, Macedonians and Grecians*, he asked her for her opinion as to who were the greater men, the ancients or her contempo-

12 Miranda to Pétion (Valenciennes, 26 October 1792) in Francisco de Miranda, *América espera* (Caracas, 1982), pp. 122–4.

raries, and was delighted when she responded indignantly that '[Benjamin] Franklin was superior to Aristides [the Just, Athenian statesman]'.[13]

Indeed, Miranda explored all types of women on his travels. It was part of his research and part of his romantic identity. He visited Philadelphia, a city whose Puritan heritage left him profoundly confused but impressed. There, Quaker women enjoyed a measure of gender equality in their households and public life that was unmatched by anything he had previously seen. In Quaker theology, the 'inner light of salvation' had no specific gender; each person was assumed to have the same powers of control over his or her behaviour. In fact, their reading of the Old Testament led believers to understand that men and women had been created equal and that the original equilibrium had been destroyed by the Fall; accordingly, a restoration of gender equality on the earthly plane would be a necessary part of humans' struggle for salvation.[14] He was fascinated to see that men and women shook hands after a Quaker meeting and addressed each other with the gender-neutral term 'friend'. Miranda frequently attended Quaker meetings, partly out of anthropological interest but also because their very austerity appealed to his own aspiring (though rarely achieved) asceticism. On Sunday 5 September, as he sat in silence for two hours at a Quaker gathering, Miranda amused himself by 'examining slowly the dress and countenances of the female concourse'. Sounding almost surprised at himself, he found that he was powerfully attracted to these women who had not a grain of powder on their faces nor a hint of perfumed oil on their bodies.[15]

Miranda often exchanged serious books with his women friends, clear evidence that he respected their intelligence and recognised their ability to enter into serious philosophical discussions. In the United States, for example, Mrs Montgomery thanked him for the loan of two books although she apologised to him that she could not return his volume of Helvetius, because she had 'absolutely fallen in love with it and cannot think of parting with it'.[16] In exchange, Mrs Montgomery hoped

13 Miranda, *New Democracy*, p. 116.

14 See the article by Karin Wulf, 'My Dear Liberty: Quaker Spinsterhood and Female Autonomy in 18th Century Pennsylvania,' in *Women and Freedom in Early America*, Larry Eldridge ed. (New York, 1997), pp. 85–93.

15 Miranda, *New Democracy*, p. 140.

16 Mrs Montgomery to Miranda, (n.p., n.d.) in *AGM*, vol. V p. 258.

he would accept a history of the revolutionary war written by an eyewitness who had lodged in her mother's house. Mrs Burr thanked Miranda for loaning her his copy of *La philosophie de la nature* [*On the Philosophy of Nature*], which 'displays strength & elegance of mind mingled with philanthropy. From his sentiments & Col. De Miranda's taste we are convinced there are souls that escape the prejudices imposed by sophistry.'[17] Miranda loved to converse with women. He enjoyed playing the part of tutor to the ones who had the shrewd sense to flatter his genius and he especially admired bright women who were knowledgeable and cultivated in languages and the fine arts. Music was one of his favourite feminine subjects of discussion. Mary Walton sent a thousand thanks to him for loaning her the major works of Rousseau which she read 'with much attention', particularly his ideas on music.[18]

The longer he stayed in the United States, the more easily Miranda was able to accustom himself to the country's social norms and use his new knowledge to advance his political goals. He always made sure to secure letters of introduction from associates in one city to their friends and relatives in another in order to smooth his entry into good society. Miranda knew how to be a good guest and, in a young republic just beginning to recover from a devastating war, the gallant, erudite, entertaining foreigner who enthusiastically admired their new system was welcomed everywhere he went. Residing in New York for more than five months, he dined with the best families, romanced their daughters and talked politics with important men. One historian has characterised Miranda as 'a champion name-dropper of his time, and he buttonholed all around him who would listen'.[19] He soon gathered an impressive pile of calling cards

17 Mrs Burr to Miranda (Tuesday Mor[nin]g), in *AGM*, vol. V, p. 259. This probably refers to the 1777 work by Jean Baptiste Claude Delisle de Sale Izouard which was popular at the time and available in both English and French editions. Similar titles included Baron Paul Henri Thierry d'Holbach's *Système de la nature* and G.W. Leibniz's *Principe de la nature et de la grâce fondés en raison. Principes de la philosophie ou Monadologie.* Natural philosophy can be traced back to St Thomas Aquinas.

18 Mary Walton to Monsieur Le Colonel Da Miranda (Mardi le matin, 6 Avril 1784), in *AGM*, vol. V, p. 265.

19 Marshall Smelser, 'George Washington Declines the Part of "El Libertador",' *William and Mary Quarterly* 11 (no. 1, January 1954), p. 45.

and invitations to dinner and those gatherings popularly known as 'dancing assemblies'. Happily, Miranda found that New Yorkers were more inclined to enjoy themselves than Philadelphians had been.

One of the major romantic relationships of Miranda's life, and certainly his first serious one, was conducted with Susan Livingston, the daughter of a wealthy and politically prominent New York family, during his US tour in 1784. At that time, Miranda was a handsome and seasoned 34-year-old soldier and Susan was a cosseted 27-year-old spinster. Along with her family's wealth and stranglehold on politics in both New York and New Jersey, Susan was pretty, well-read, unconventional and fatally attracted to danger, a combination that Miranda found difficult to resist. Their courtship began typically enough through an exchange of books, the older man taking on the role of tutor and loaning the younger woman copies of works by two of his favourite authors: David Hume and the Abbé Raynal. Coquettishly, Susan sent him little notes of thanks, flattering his brilliant choices and expressing her gratitude for exposure to such sublime ideas. In early January 1784, Susan's interest in the mysterious foreigner had become serious enough to write to him on behalf of her friends who 'take a *great* interest in all that concerns you, & wish to have a particular information of your *political situation* [as] there are some things *insinuated* that are not in the least advantageous to *your* honor'.[20] She had heard that he was a wanted man, a deserter from the Spanish service, a circumstance that was creating opposition to their deepening relationship among her friends and family. For her part, Susan appeared to be undeterred by the transgression; as a woman, one of the few public stands in support of political liberty that she could make was her choice of husband; a fugitive from the tyrannical Spanish monarchy would be just such a statement. If the man himself happened to be handsome and charismatic, so much the better. Over the next months, Susan's letters to Miranda became longer and more intimate and eventually had to be delivered through a trusted courier. Their special friendship was an open secret, however, causing some in her circle to joke that young Miss Livingston was destined to become the 'Queen of the Incas'.[21]

20 Susan Livingston to Miranda ([New York], 10 January 1784) in *AGM*, vol. XIII, pp. 200–01.

21 The actual reference is found in Susan Livingston to Miranda (Hanover Square [New York], 1785), *AGM*, vol. XIII, pp. 214–15 in which she said

Susan's sisters and girlfriends, however, rejected such a prospect out of hand and never lost a chance to sabotage the relationship. They found Miranda absurd and pretentious at the very least, and thought his unstable life was unacceptable for their dear Susan. Eventually, some of them became concerned that the impetuous woman might have written letters to her sweetheart which might compromise her reputation or her future. Her girlfriends raided Miranda's guest room during one of his frequent absences from New York and apparently went so far as to break open his trunks so that they could rummage through his books and papers to search for any incriminating evidence. Upon returning and finding his things in disarray, Miranda quarrelled with the invaders, vociferously denying that any inappropriate relationship with Miss Livingston had existed. As he told the girls, 'he requires three months acquaintance with a lady before he enters into conversation with them to avoid the great error of not adapting to the idea & turn of the lady'.[22] That comment was disingenuous at best and it certainly did not fool Sarah's self-appointed protectresses. Months later, when Miranda left Susan in New York while he went on a tour of Europe, Susan's cousin Sarah Vaughan declared herself pleased that Miranda had finally departed the country and did not 'venerate his character sufficiently to wish his return'. He carried Susan's memory along with him, but left no firm evidence of any promise or betrothal made between them.

The next major relationship that Francisco de Miranda built with a woman was one of a very different nature. After two years spent travelling through northern Europe, Italy, Greece and Turkey, Miranda decided to venture northward through Russia to study that dynamic empire which had recently added the Crimea and Alaska to its territories. Through his friendship with Prince Potemkin, Francisco de Miranda met Russia's Empress Catherine the Great in Kiev on Valentine's Day 1787, at precisely 11:30 a.m. As a gentleman, the young

---

'perhaps you will understand their allusion, I do not'. Both José Nucete-Sardi, *Aventura y tragedia de Francisco de Miranda* (Barcelona, 1971), p. 31; and William Spence Robertson, *The Life of Miranda* (New York, 1969), vol. I, p. 44, attributed the letter to Eliza Livingston, her sister, but the copy in Miranda's archive seems to be written by Susan herself.

22 Sarah Vaughan to H.W. Livingston (Thursday 25 [November 1784]) in *Massachusetts Historical Society, Matthew Ridley Papers.*

man bent to kiss her hand, but as a republican Miranda recorded in his diary for posterity that he had not fallen all over himself to 'genuflect in front of royalty'.[23] Catherine took an immediate interest in the handsome stranger and invited him to join her evening meal. Her attentions flattered Miranda, of course, but he also appreciated her intelligence and the 'goodness and excellence of her [h]eart.' He had heard through court gossips that the Empress found him to be 'sincere and learned, exactly the type of man that she liked'.[24]

At each subsequent meeting, their conversations rambled over a wide range of topics: the Inquisition, North Africa's garrisons and culture, European literature, Russian history, Miranda's travels and the people he had met. Before long, rumours of a more intimate relationship between the two began to surface. Two years later, in 1789, Miranda's erstwhile friend the US-based speculator Stephen Sayre leered (and half-lamented) that he had heard that Miranda 'had travelled to great advantage, nothing has escaped his *penetration*, not even the Empress of all the Russias, I believe — a mortifying *declaration* for me to make, who was 21 months in her Capital, without ever making myself acquainted with the internal parts of *her extensive and well-known Dominions*'.[25] Thomas Paine, too, recalled that '[Miranda] did not tell me of his affair with old Catharine [sic] of Russia, nor did I tell him that I knew of it.'[26] Yet most historians agree that a physical relationship between the two was unlikely.[27] Although Catherine was well known for her many lovers, she tended to be serially monogamous and was involved with the dashing Count Dmitri Mamonov at the time. Furthermore, the Empress was 58 years old when they met, Miranda was just 36, and he himself described her love for him as 'the affection of a mother'.[28] Nevertheless, their relationship was intense

23 Miranda, 'Viajes por Grecia, Turquía y Rusia,' *AGM*, vol. II, p. 258.

24 *Ibid.*

25 Stephen Sayre to Samuel Ogden (London, 29 June 1789), *Massachusetts Historical Society, Henry Knox Papers, reel 24, #70*. Sayre's emphasis as underlined in the original.

26 Thomas Paine to [unknown] (New Rochelle, 20 March 1806), in *The Complete Writings of Thomas Paine*, Philip S. Foner, ed. (New York, 1945), pp. 1480–2.

27 Madariaga, *Travels*, p. 12; Thorning, *World Citizen*, p. 61; Angel Grisanti, *Miranda y la Emperatriz Catalina la Grande* (Caracas, 1928), p. 6.

28 Miranda, *XVIIIth Century Diary*, p. 98.

enough to provoke Potemkin's jealousy and Miranda's former friend and protector began to try to hurry the foreigner on his way.

Empress Catherine and Francisco de Miranda's interest in each other was more than just a pleasant personal diversion. For both of them, their relationship offered the promise of real material or political advantage. At the exact moment that Miranda arrived in the Russian court, explorer Grigorii Shelikov returned from Irkutsk to report that he had founded a commercial settlement on Alaska's Kodiak Island. Catherine and her advisers, it seems, were debating the possibility of expanding the Russian Empire eastward from Siberia into North America. The recent discovery of valuable sea otters in the Aleutian Islands had attracted her attention and suggested the need for a more serious and visible Russian presence in the Americas. Catherine's pointed questions about the nature and strength of the Spanish presence in America, therefore, were not disinterested. For his part, Miranda understood that he too had something to gain from the Russian Empress's expansionist national agenda. If Miranda wished to initiate a movement for Spanish American emancipation, it was clear to him that he would need to have the backing of at least one major international power, both to provide funds and supplies and to exert diplomatic pressure. Both sides wondered if the other would be a useful ally in their respective political projects. Always circumspect in his diary for fear of self-incrimination, should they be captured, Miranda evidently talked with Potemkin, Mamonov and Catherine herself about 'it', undoubtedly a cryptic allusion to his plans to revolutionise South America. On 12 April 1787, Mamonov reported to Miranda that the Empress had sanctioned his plans, saying '[t]hat my way of thinking appeared to her to be very good … that as she did not know the *place* [Venezuela] she was not able to give me counsel as to the execution [of the plans] but that later she would tell me more in regard to the matter'.[29]

He spent much of his time in Russia talking about America, not just with Catherine, but with others as well. Although the two had not met before, French envoy Louis-Philippe, the Count de Ségur, had toured the United States in 1783; furthermore, as a youth Ségur had spent four days in Caracas and so the two were able to exchange fond remem-

29 *Ibid.*, p. 100.

brances of both places.[30] Like Miranda, Ségur too had known the Arestiguieta family in Caracas, and remembered Miss Bowen and Miss P[olly] Scott in Boston. Imagine, thought Miranda, to come all the way to Russia, 'only to find here men who have been in my house!' Personal relationships formed in drawing rooms and politicised salons operated by patriotic women throughout the Atlantic world in the age of revolution did much to link the cause of liberty on both sides of the ocean.

For his part, Ségur described Miranda as 'a well-educated and spiritual man, audacious and given to intrigue'.[31] The cynical Frenchman was amazed at the way Miranda had persuaded the Russian Empress that he was 'a martyr to philosophy, and a victim of the Inquisition'. Miranda recorded proudly in his diary that Ségur once told him that the gallant Venezuelan 'was a great courtier, as in a short time I had been able to make the Sovereign take an interest in me, when she did not address a single word during a month to many foreigners of note'.[32] His secret weapons may have been his respect for women's abilities and his ability to engage Catherine in practical political talk. Although the Russian Empire had been unique in the feminisation of its leadership in the eighteenth century, jealous Russian noblemen and their continental counterparts never completely accepted this unnatural order of things.[33] Miranda, on the other hand, delighted in Catherine's power and she, in turn, showered him with attention and unfailing support for his plans.

Eventually, the protestations of Ambassador Normandez reached Catherine's ear and warned her about the imprudence of openly flouting the Spanish King's wishes by harbouring a fugitive. On 29 March 1787, Catherine asked Miranda to give up any idea of returning to his homeland, where he was sure to be persecuted for his ideas; instead, she suggested, why not join her court permanently with a handsome state

30 *Mémoires ou Souvenirs et Anecdotes par M. Le Comte de Ségur* (Paris, 1825), p. 425; Carlos Duarte (ed.), *Misión secreta en Puerto Cabello y viaje á Caracas en 1783* (Caracas, 1991), p. 301; Miranda, 'Viajes por Grecia, Turquía y Rusia,' *AGM*, vol. II, p. 268.

31 Ségur, *Souvenirs et Anecdotes*, pp. 63–5.

32 Miranda, *XVIIIth Century Diary*, p. 94.

33 Natalia Pushkareva, *Women in Russian History*, translated by Eve Levin (London, 1997), especially Chapter Three, 'Women in the Enlightenment,' pp 121–69.

salary, a title and a furnished home? Naturally the offer flattered Miranda, who replied that while there was no one who 'loved the Empress more than I … surely the thing is impossible'.[34] He explained to her that [o]nly a great and interesting matter such as the one that presently occupies my attention would be able to make me decline the sweet and agreeable pleasure of being able to repay you with my services for all that which I owe to Your Majesty's benevolence …[35]

Catherine refused to hand over her pet to the Spaniards, however; instead, she put an end to the controversy by bestowing on him the Russian title of Count Miranda, granting him 10,000 roubles and guaranteeing him the protection of her Imperial Embassies throughout Europe if he should ever have need of their services. Miranda later fondly recalled that the Empress had told him that 'if the Spanish Empire was in danger on my account, I could be in no better place than in Russia as it was the most distant from Spain than any country — and that as regards the feeling which her Majesty had for me it had nothing to do with the rank I had in Spain but was due my personal qualities'.[36] With this, there was little more that Normandez and Macañaz could do except to grumble and pass the disturbing information on to Madrid. A strong woman had saved Miranda from a Spanish jail and made it possible for him to travel with a greater measure of personal security than ever before. He never forgot her generosity and steely nerves and could never be persuaded that women were inferior to men in their public or political capacities.

And so, Miranda left Russia and spent nearly two more decades seeking support for his lifelong dream of liberating his native America. He travelled ever onward, sheltered and cared for by women along the way. Most of these relationships were innocent extensions of hospitality in a domestic setting. Occasionally, they spilled over into something more. After his doomed romantic relationship with Susan Livingston and his political friendship with Russia's Catherine the Great, Miranda's next major emotional involvement came upon him unexpectedly while visiting Norway and Sweden in November 1787. He was, as usual, touring

34 Miranda, 'Viajes por Grecia, Turquía y Rusia,' *AGM*, vol. II, p. 298.

35 Miranda to Emperatriz Catalina II (San Petersburgo, 15 August 1787) in *América espera*, p. 91.

36 Miranda, *XVIIIth Century Diary*, p. 110.

libraries, military establishments, mines, ports and forests, hoping to learn useful information for his own future nation. Miranda was impressed with Scandinavia, saying that '[i]t is a noteworthy thing to see the degree of civilisation, of instruction and elegance in which these people here live ... it is the result of commerce and communication which they have with England and Holland'.[37] He found the strong, tall, blonde-haired, blue-eyed Nordic women to be very good-looking and happily accepted a list of 'Nymphs of Cythera' [referring to the ancient centre for the cult of Aphrodite] that Count de Ranzau had given him for his paid pleasure.

In Gothenburg, however, Miranda met an English expatriate named Catherine Hall and by all accounts he fell deeply in love with her. The matter was complicated since she ardently reciprocated his affections but unfortunately was already married to a wealthy British merchant. At the end of December 1787 Miranda noted in his diary that he lunched with the captivating Catherine, 'who is very upsetting to me ... after cultivating a little tenderness, which I note is beginning to appear, I went home to write'.[38] The affair was conducted passionately under the cuckolded husband's nose, although Mrs Hall's servants were aware of the deception. Miranda and Catherine took any excuse they could find to venture out together for many long private carriage rides during which they exchanged a thousand kisses and, in all likelihood, something more. On one amorous expedition, their coachman purposely made the carriage lurch, Miranda snarled, '*so that it was most embarrassing*' for the lovers. Another time, a knock on their door from some unexpected French visitors interrupted the lovers 'in their bliss'. Eventually Miranda realised that he must extract himself from an impossible situation, despite the pain to both involved, but not before they vowed to sustain their love through frequent letters. Catherine gave Miranda her silhouette in a locket along with a snippet of her golden hair; in exchange, she took one of his brooches and promised to wear it on her breast forever. The tragic (or tawdry) month-long affair might have ended there, but for a possible footnote of historical significance; rumours still persist that Miranda conceived the colour scheme for the independent Venezuelan flag from the face of his beloved Catherine Hall: yellow for her hair, blue for her eyes, red for her lips.

37 *Ibid.*, p. 129.
38 *Ibid.*, p. 130.

Miranda's life was difficult, watching over his shoulder for the Spanish spies who dogged him persistently. He occasionally found solace in the arms and beds of women along the way, but his dangerous, transient lifestyle precluded the formation of any real deep relationships. Not surprisingly, his mind often wandered back to happier times. When ages passed with no word from America Miranda was sincerely hurt, asking why 'not one of my friends in that part of the world shows atention [sic] it seems, to this part of the old'. Eventually Henry Knox replied, sending warm greetings and passing on the delicate news that the letter Miranda had enclosed for 'his female friend', probably Susan Livingston, was being returned to him because as a married woman she 'conceived her situation rendered it improper' to correspond with other men. She still professed a sincere friendship for Miranda, if that was some small consolation for him.[39] The lonely man felt dismayed and began to realise the great personal sacrifice that his commitment to Spanish American emancipation had exacted. He was 40 years old, had no permanent home, no real profession and no steady income.

The situation did not change for another decade. By 1805 Miranda had resided outside South America for a longer time than he had actually lived there. The great project of Spanish American emancipation had been his surrogate family for over two decades. Young, impressionable men like the future liberator of Chile Bernardo O'Higgins had sought his counsel in London and took the place of the sons he never had.[40] Yet at the age of 55, he was beginning to tire of being alone; it might have been exciting for a youthful adventurer, but was decidedly less appealing for an ageing adult. Miranda wanted to escape his lonely existence in a never-ending series of rented lodgings and put down more permanent roots. With the aid of friends, he bought a house at 27 Grafton Street in a fashionable West End neighbourhood near the newly-established British Museum.[41] It was to this three-storey

39 Knox to Miranda, (New York, 5 September 1790), *MHS*, *Knox Papers*, reel 26, no. 177.

40 O'Higgins recalled that Miranda referred to him as 'my son' in Bernardo O'Higgins, *Epistolario O'Higgins 1798–1819* (Madrid, 1920), vol. I, pp. 29n–30n.

41 Miranda and his wife Sarah Andrews were the third occupants of the house which was built in 1792. In 1978, the Venezuelan government bought the

Georgian-style home that he brought his new wife Sarah Andrews, a young woman he had met on a tour of northern England.[42] Very little is known about Sarah, except that she came from a rural family and that she was the niece of the famous London portrait painter Stephen Hewson. Some historians have claimed that Sarah was Jewish, although there is no firm evidence for that characterisation. Similarly, no marriage certificate has ever been found to document the vows between Miranda and Sarah, but extensive investigations by Venezuela's former cultural attaché in London, Miriam Blanco Fombona de Hood, seem to prove that Miranda and Sarah did not simply cohabit but were actually legally married. The first of their two sons, Leandro, was born on 9 October 1803 shortly after the happy couple moved into Grafton Street and Miranda settled into a satisfying domestic life at long last.

Although he was 55 years old and took great pleasure in his young family, Miranda kept his dream for Spanish American emancipation firmly at the forefront of his activities. He could not break his lifelong habit of revolutionising, even for the longed-for comforts of home and hearth. In 1805 he departed for the United States where he put together an expedition to Coro, Venezuela, that ended in disaster in 1806. Although the expedition's failure can be attributed to many factors, including bad advance information, a hostile local populace and insufficient supplies, General Miranda's preoccupation with his own health and the state of his young family back in London greatly undermined his effectiveness as a leader and damaged his reputation among the men.

After decades spent preparing for this prodigal return to Venezuela, Miranda was actually homesick for England; that unexpected sentiment was perhaps the best evidence of the conflicted state of his national identity. Tellingly, Miranda did not name his vessel after an American person or place, or with a typical reference to a classical hero or lofty

---

house and converted it into the seat of their cultural mission. For the physical structure's history see: Guido Acuña, *La casa de Miranda en Londres* (México DF, 1979); José Salcedo-Bastardo, *Crucible of Americanism: Miranda's London House* (Caracas, 1981); and Miriam Blanco Fombona de Hood, *La casa de Miranda en Londres: Cómo fue adquirida por Venezuela* (Caracas, 1981a).

42 Miriam Blanco Fombona de Hood, *El enigma de Sarah Andrews, Esposa de Francisco de Miranda* (Caracas, 1981). Carlos Pi Sunyer, *Patriotas americanos en Londres* (Caracas, 1978), pp. 69, 81.

concept, rather he christened it the *Leander*, in English, after his three-year-old British son. There were a million details that required his immediate attention, yet he still found the time to write frequent and long letters to Vansittart, John Turnbull and his wife Sarah, instructing them in the conduct of his affairs back home. Miranda explicitly told Turnbull that he wanted Leandro to be baptised by a Roman Catholic priest but that it should be done without much fanfare and with the consent of the boy's mother.[43] There remains a particularly touching correspondence between Miranda and his young wife, who gave birth to their second son Francisco *hijo* [junior] while the father-general was away in the United States. Calling him 'My ever dearest G', Sarah kept Miranda informed of every detail of her daily life with the children, from bricklayers' fees to Leandro's charming antics. One of her favourite pastimes was watching when

> [Leandro] getts the newspaper and setts down for some time as if he were reading, and then asks for a pen and ink to coppy it out, for thay is very good news of papa, papa is at C[or]o, and I am going, he will send a ship for me, and I shall be a G[enera]l with papa.[44]

Precocious little Leandro undoubtedly learned this game by watching his equally devoted mother compile a scrapbook of articles relating to Miranda's expedition clipped from London's popular press.

Life was not easy for Sarah during Miranda's absence. Sarah worried constantly about money, staved off an attempt by the Dulau booksellers to repossess her husband's prized library and thwarted the occasional swindler anxious to take advantage of an unprotected woman. Most of all, Sarah was intensely lonely; she even considered taking her boys to the United States because, as she wrote her husband

> without you life is become insuportable, your dear letter and my Leandr are the only consolation I can find in the midst of my trubbles my lovly children God pray them I often pray for them

43 Miranda to Turnbull (Nueva York, 4 January 1806) in *Testigos norteamericanos de la expedición de Miranda (Sherman, Smith, Ingersoll)*, Edgardo Mondolfi, ed. (Caracas, 1992) p. 177.

44 Sarah [Andrews] Martin to Francisco Miranda (London, 9 February 1807), *AGM*, vol. XIX, pp. 76–8.

> to be in Heven then to live in this dispiseable world — I hope one grave will contain us all and not live to feel the pangs of misery that I am forst to feel.[45]

She begged him to 'wright soon my ever dear sir, that is the only consolation I have, reading over and over your dear letter and the hopes of soon meething again'.[46] Sarah Andrews, like other women of her class and era, did not receive a sophisticated education; her handwriting was shaky and her command of spelling and grammar weak, but the intensity of her feelings for Miranda and her children is unmistakable. Despite her literary shortcomings, Sarah Andrews exerted great effort to write long, informative, frequent letters to her faraway husband. For his part, Miranda kept his young family's welfare close to his heart. He implored his influential friends the chancellor of the exchequer Nicholas Vansittart and merchant John Turnbull to guard over them in his absence and used these men as trusted conduits for his letters back home.[47] When Miranda docked at Portsmouth on 31 December 1807 he had a real home to which he could return.

His happy domestic circumstances notwithstanding, Miranda acted like other men of his age by engaging in discreet extramarital relationships. He had chosen a wife whose steadfastness and loyalty could not be questioned, but whose intellectual achievements could not satisfy him. In 1809 the married father of two encountered the woman who was the last great love affair of his life. Lady Hester Lucy Stanhope was the brilliant but erratic 27-year-old niece of William Pitt the Younger. Lady Hester had come from a stifling country estate to London in 1803 to serve as her unmarried uncle's social hostess and had quickly shocked polite society with her unconventional ways of dress and behaviour.[48]

45 [Sarah Andrews] to Francisco Miranda (London, 20 June 1807) in *AGM*, vol. XIX, pp. 130–4.

46 Sarah Andrews to Francisco Miranda (London, 4 July 1807) *AGM*, vol. XIX, pp. 134–8.

47 See, as examples, Miranda to Nicholas Vansittart (Aruba, 19 September 1806) *AGM*, vol. XVIII, pp. 171–2; Miranda to John Turnbull (Trinidad, 10 June 1807); and Miranda to Vansittart (Trinidad, 10 June 1807) both in *AGM*, vol. XIX, pp. 50–1, 53.

48 See Virginia Childs, *Lady Hester Stanhope: Queen of the Desert* (London, 1990) and Alberto Miramón, *La llama que no muere* (Caracas, 1983).

For his part, the indulgent Pitt enjoyed Lady Hester's outrageousness and took pleasure in introducing her to the most pompous and self-important people he could find, sure that some great anecdote would result; his obliging niece rarely disappointed him in that respect. Before meeting Miranda, she had suffered several intense and embarrassingly public entanglements with prominent society gentlemen, most notably Sir Granville Leveson-Gower and Sir John Moore. Lady Hester was ripe for another romantic adventure when friends introduced her to the notorious Venezuelan general Francisco de Miranda in April 1809.

From that date onward, the pair dined together frequently. Always captivated by bright women, Miranda recorded in his diary that Lady Hester offered the most lovely, erudite and liberal conversation ranging over several subjects. She professed to be devoted to the cause of Venezuelan independence under a system of rational liberty and was most anxious to visit that interesting country herself. In fact, Stanhope told him that she planned to emigrate to Caracas and open a school for girls. Miranda was immediately besotted. He declared her to be one of the most interesting women he had ever met and despaired to learn that she was setting out for Wales the next day to take the country air for her health. Ever the coquette, before she left London Lady Hester found the time to send a copy of Sydney Smith's recent edition of the *Letters of Peter Plymly* to the handsome foreigner accompanied with an open invitation to visit her when she returned to the city in ten days.[49]

It should not be surprising that the unconventional couple found each other attractive. By all accounts Lady Hester was a woman who was 'always happiest in the company of men, preferably those that were handsome, intelligent and half in love with her' and Miranda was all three.[50] Calling her 'the most delicious woman I have yet encountered', Lady Hester Stanhope was, for a time, the Cleopatra to Miranda's Caesar.[51]

49 Thorning claims that the two met in October, *World Citizen*, p. 202; Miramón cites Miranda's diary entries and gives the date as April 1809, *La llama*, pp. 20–21.

50 Childs, *Lady Hester Stanhope*, p. 15. She herself frequently referred to a 'general want of sympathy toward her own sex' whom she generally viewed as silly, vain or stupid, and very often all three. *Memoirs of Lady Hester Stanhope*, 3 vols. (Austria, 1985), vol. I, p. 84.

51 Miramón, *La llama*, pp. 39, 45.

Although rumours persist among Miranda's South American biographers that Lady Hester was the true mother of one, or both, of his sons, the late date of their acquaintance seems to preclude the possibility.[52] This rumour draws its strength from not only from the relationship between Lady Hester and Francisco Miranda, which surely existed as an intense intellectual friendship, but also from her continued interest in the education and welfare of the Miranda boys well into the 1820s. Although she left Britain permanently in February 1810, Lady Hester kept in touch with the general's family and later brought Leandro, possibly even Francisco as well, out to visit her in Lebanon.

In July and August 1809 Miranda travelled throughout the English countryside, partly to visit friends like James Mill who had invited him to Oxted at Jeremy Bentham's request, partly to join in the traditional English summer activities and partly to continue building his useful connections.[53] Nicholas Vansittart had hinted that it might be a good idea for Miranda to get out of the city for a while. The Spanish Embassy's attaché Juan Ruiz de Apodaca had been complaining loudly that the notorious Venezuelan continued to engage in subterfuge by corresponding with other known South American patriots like Argentine Saturnino Rodríguez Peña and others. No doubt Miranda's decision to take some country air was nudged along by the removal of Lady Hester to her summer house at Bath. On his way to visit Mill, Miranda casually stopped by to spend some time with her, discreetly taking lodgings in an inn next to her home. The two rode horses, dined together and met furtively in the evenings.

The year 1810 was momentous for Spanish America politically and for Francisco de Miranda personally. In that year, Spanish Americans in Buenos Aires and Caracas rose in defiance of Napoleon's takeover of

52 J.A. Cova, 'Intimidades de don Francisco de Miranda,' *Boletín de la Academia Nacional de Historia* 33 (no. 130, April–June 1950), p. 177; William Robertson, *Rise of the Spanish American Republics* (New York, 1946), p. 79 followed historian Ricardo Becerra and agreed that Miranda's children were born of Sarah Andrews. Carlos Villanueva interpreted an 1850 letter by Leandro Miranda alluding to an inheritance from Lady Hester as proof that she was his mother. In fact, Lady Hester died penniless in Lebanon and had no fortune to leave anyone, son or not, Stanhope, *Memoirs,* vol. III, pp. 338–40.

53 J.R. Dinwiddy, 'Bentham's Transition to Political Radicalism 1809–1810,' *Journal of the History of Ideas*, 36 (no. 4, October–December 1975), p. 686.

the Spanish throne. As the Napoleonic Wars spread and placed an ever-greater demand on British resources, Lady Hester Stanhope became so disillusioned with the conservative nature of English politics that she vowed to leave her homeland forever. Miranda wrote to her, his 'dear and beloved Lady Hester', expressing a fervent wish that the superiority of her spirit would carry her far beyond the petty troubles in which she had become embroiled. He assured her that he considered her 'irreplaceable', both as a lover and as an intelligent adviser. Indeed, his commitment to liberal causes found its counterpart in his modern approach to his woman friend. In one of their last exchanges Miranda recounted for Hester his recent interviews with English parliamentarian and abolitionist William Wilberforce and the Duke of Gloucester, wishing that she could be near in order to discuss these events with him and offer her sage counsel.[54] Lady Hester departed on the frigate *Jason* at the end of January 1810, requesting that her dear general should direct future letters to her under cover to General Torrens of the Horse Guards who would make sure that they reached her safely. He probably never saw her again.

Sarah Andrews kept her head high and tended the home front for Miranda. She kept the candles perpetually lit at Grafton Street, symbolising the general's open door for all disaffected Spanish American patriots who cared to seek refuge there. In summer 1810 a Venezuelan delegation comprised of university administrator Luis López Méndez, government secretary Andrés Bello and aristocratic gadabout Simón Bolívar stayed for nearly two months while they petitioned the British government for political recognition; Argentine Matías Yrigoyen arrived at the same time with a similar commission. He agreed to return to Caracas to aid the new patriot government in late 1810, but before he left, Miranda added a codicil to his 1805 will. He designated Vansittart and Turnbull as his executors and left the bulk of his property to his wife Sarah Andrews and their two sons. When the appointed departure date arrived, Miranda kissed his family goodbye, trying hard to ignore Sarah's tears and promising her that they would be reunited again very soon. She did not relish the thought of another long separation, this time having to survive as a single parent of two small children trying to

54 Miranda to Stanhope (Grafton Street, 21 January 1810), reprinted in Miramón, *La llama,* pp. 45–6.

make ends meet on a very small income. Once again, Miranda's patriotic dreams overrode his personal attachments and he sailed away with dreams of liberation before his eyes.

He was less welcome in Venezuela than he could have imagined. The Caracas junta was trying to steer a middle course, remaining outwardly loyal to King Ferdinand while laying the groundwork for full independence at some indeterminate date. Miranda, a generation older than these men, exhibited a more liberated mentality. Under the general's influence, at the end of the year 1810 a group of engaged politicians and intellectuals founded the Patriotic Club, a sort of Jacobin-styled discussion group intended to build solidarity and to raise political consciousness.[55] Right from its inception, the Patriotic Club appeared dangerously radical to those who feared a full-blown revolution in Caracas. For one thing, its meetings were held in the poorer parts of town and its membership was open to anyone who shared the group's sympathies: both the old and the young, women, mulattos, blacks and Indians. Under Miranda's leadership, the Club agitated vigorously for full independence and started to produce its own serial publication *El Patriota Venezolano*. Opponents tried to tar the Club with the Jacobin brush, claiming that it had many French members and aimed to subvert the moderate government with its wild agenda.[56] As he had done years ago in France, Miranda advocated a public role for women which not only would reflect their significant economic power, but also would be more consistent with the notions of liberty as he understood them.

While in Venezuela, Miranda engaged in correspondence with several women of different classes.[57] Several letters mention his violence and rebuke his seeming indifference to the woman's devotion. One upper-class lady with cultivated penmanship asked him to 'pardon my tyranny

55 [Manuel Palacio Fajardo], *Outline of the Revolution in Spanish America* (New York, 1817), p. 73. Francisco Espejo seconded Miranda's proposal for the club.

56 Robert Semple, *Sketch of the Present State of Caracas* (London, 1812), pp. 127–8.

57 For a rare discussion of women in the wars of independence, see Evelyn Cherpak, 'The Participation of Women in the Independence Movement in Gran Colombia 1870–1830,' in Asunción Lavrín (ed.), *Latin American Women*, (Westport, CT, 1978).

and cruelty, which was born more of your violence than of my own will'.[58] In another letter, the same woman begged to be allowed to prostrate herself at his feet and beg his forgiveness for undescribed transgressions. In two letters, Teresa Otalora listed the number of shirts, pants, shoes and pesos that she was donating to General Miranda's expedition against the resurgent Spanish royalists. A woman purporting to be his cousin María Jonte de Miranda addressed him with the republican salutation 'Citizen' and sent her son Vicente to join the patriot cause.[59] In fact, ample evidence exists that Miranda actively courted women as a natural and logical constituency for his republic of liberty in America. It was not enough. His forces could not withstand the royalist onslaught and Miranda capitulated to Spanish commander Domingo Monteverde. Instead of being permitted to return to Sarah and his comfortable life in London, Miranda was seized and taken to the notorious Spanish jail in La Carraca. He never breathed free air again.

During the last four pitiful years of his life, Miranda again owed much of his comfort and survival to a woman. There is some speculation that the mysterious woman who visited Miranda occasionally and provided financial aid while he was in La Carraca using the name of *señorita* Leonor de Flores was none other than Lady Hester Lucy Stanhope herself. Letters addressed to *señorita* Leonor de Flores were sent to Calle de San Cristobal in the Isla de León and subsequently to the Calle de San Francisco de Asís. Perhaps not coincidentally, it is true that Hester Stanhope was known to be travelling throughout Europe at that time and she did not head eastward to settle in the Middle East until the winter of 1816, after Miranda's death occurred.[60] There is no question that Lady Hester retained a lifelong attachment to the man and his family. In her will, she left one of her most treasured possessions, Lord Chatham's seal, to General Miranda's heirs.[61] Plots to effect the elderly general's escape swirled around all him. In April 1816, Turnbull had advanced £266 to some shady characters who had promised to spirit the

58 [Anonymous] to Miranda [1812], *Great Britain, National Maritime Museum, MS 83/045.*

59 María Jonte de Miranda to Francisco de Miranda (Vega, 11 June 1812), *National Maritime Museum MS 83/045.*

60 Miramón, *La llama*, pp. 50–1.

61 Thorning, *World Citizen*, p. 206.

general out of his cell and deliver him safely to the arms of his British protectors in Gibraltar.[62] Using the good offices of the mysterious *señorita* at the Isla de León, the rest of the money found its way into the right hands and the final details for Miranda's escape were hammered out. Alas, just as they appeared to be arriving at the point of success, the conspirators' scheme was cut short by the unforeseen circumstance of Miranda's rapidly deteriorating health. He suffered a cerebral haemorrhage and died a few days later on 14 July 1816.

Francisco de Miranda was a man caught between centuries and between cultures. As a multilingual citizen of the Atlantic world, Miranda's true country was liberty. He had only one idea; all his attitudes and actions sprang from the notion that human society was progressing from tyranny to liberty. In the context of international politics, this conviction explains Miranda's single-minded devotion to the cause of Spanish American emancipation which lasted for 40 years on four different continents. On a more intimate level, Miranda followed the more radical position of Enlightenment authors like Condorcet in advocating full political rights for women as a logical extension of the concept of liberty itself. He liked women and he respected their intelligence. Through his personal experiences with Russia's powerful and capable Empress Catherine the Great, he knew that women could lead great nations. He denounced the hypocrisy of men who worshipped at the temple of equality but preferred to remain tyrants in their own homes. At the same time, when Miranda finally settled into married life, he chose Sarah Andrews as his wife, a young, simple, barely-literate country girl, not someone who would represent a more equal intellectual or social match. It seems he did not entirely escape the desire to be dominant.

Francisco de Miranda, however, did view his relationships with women as part of his trans-Atlantic struggle on behalf of liberty. He engaged women intellectually, investigated subcultures like the Quakers who might offer alternative models for female participation in public life, and also suggested practical measures for their elevation when he could. In 1792 Miranda advocated the extension of voting rights to women with property; 20 years later he was still fighting on their behalf when he welcomed women members into the Patriotic Club in Caracas.

62 Turnbull to [Vansittart] (Gibraltar, 8 April 1816), British Library, *Add. MSS 31,232, f.43.*

By treating them respectfully and listening to their opinions, he was able to flatter their underutilised intelligence and thereby use them as conduits to reach their husbands, fathers and sons. His strategy was not entirely self-serving, however. Women always represented Miranda's most natural and best constituency. He condemned male licentiousness that spawned illegitimate children and left families unsupported. He advocated better and more modern education for women not only as a way to raise up better republican children but also as a way to reach their own potential as individuals. For Miranda, his life's works and his many loves were intimately connected. He understood that the advance of liberty in one sphere naturally bolstered its chances in another. He did not codify his thought in a formal treatise, but his attitudes toward women, liberation and the way of the future can be discerned in all his activities. He was after love in an era of liberation. To the mind of a man of action, liberty was a project that one gender alone could not conceive; any attempt to do so, would only result in a still birth.

Bibliography

Acuña, Guido (1979) *La casa de Miranda en Londres*, (México DF: Imprenta Madero SA)

Alexander, James T. (1989) *Catherine the Great: Life and Legend* (New York: Oxford University Press).

Anon (1780) *Le Soldat Citoyen, ou Vues patriotiques sur la manière la plus avantageuse de pourvoir a la défense du royaume*, Dans le Pays de la Liberté [Neuchatel], 1780.

Antepara, José María (1810) *South American Emancipation. Documents Historical and Explanatory, Shewing the Designs which have been in Progress and the Exertions made by General Miranda, for the Attainment of that Object during the last Twenty-Five Years* (London).

Archivo del General Miranda (original). three sections: *Viajes* (1764-1793); *Revolución Francesa* (1792-1808); and *Negociaciones* (1770-1810).

Barbier, Patrick (1990) *Historia de los Castrati* (Buenos Aires: Javier Vergara Editor).

Baylen, Joseph and Woodward, Dorothy (1950) 'Francisco de Miranda and Russian Diplomacy 1787–1788,' *The Historian*, vol. 13, pp. 52–68.

Berruezo León, María Teresa (1989) *La lucha de Hispanoamérica por su independencia en Inglaterra, 1800-1830* (Madrid).

Bierck, Jr., Harold A. (1955) 'The First Instance of U.S. Foreign Aid: Venezuelan Relief in 1812,' *Inter-American Economic Affairs*, vol. IX, no. 1 (Summer), pp. 47-59.

Blanco Fombona de Hood, Miriam (1981) *El enigma de Sarah Andrews, esposa de Francisco de Miranda* (Caracas: Instituto de Investigaciones Históricas de la Universidad Católica Andrés Bello).

Blanco Fombona de Hood, Miriam (1981a) *La casa de Miranda en Londres: Cómo fue adquirida por Venezuela* (Caracas: Instituto de Investigaciones Históricas de la Universidad Católica Andrés Bello).

Bolívar, Simón (1951) *Selected writings*; compiled by Vicente Lecuna, edited by Harold A. Bierck, Jr., translation by Lewis Bertrand, 2. vols. (New York: The Colonial Press Inc.).

Briceño Iragorry, Mario (1983) *Discursos académicos y tribuna patria e historia* (Caracas: Biblioteca de Temas y Autores Trujillanos), no. 10.

Burke, William (James Mill) (1807) *South American Independence: or, the Emancipation of South America, the Glory and Interest of England* (London).

Burke, William (James Mill) (1808) *Additional Reasons for Our Immediately Emancipating Spanish America* (2nd edn., London).

Calcaño, José Antonio (1985) *La ciudad y su música. Crónica musical de Caracas* (Caracas: Monte Avila Editores), Colección Letra y Solfa.

Calzavara, Alberto (1986) *Historia de la música en Venezuela. Período Hispánico con referencias al teatro y la danza* (Caracas: Fundación Pampero).

Castillo Didier, Miguel (1984) 'El Precursor Francisco de Miranda y la música,' in *Revista Musical de Venezuela,* Caracas, year 5, nos. 12–14 (January–December), pp. 101–2.

Catherine II, Empress of Russia (1927) *Memoirs of Catherine the Great,* Katherine Anthony, translator (New York: Alfred A. Knopf).

Cazotte, Jacques (2000) *Miranda 1750–1816: Histoire de un séducteur* (Paris: Perrin).

Cherpak, Evelyn (1978) 'The Participation of Women in the Independence Movement in Gran Colombia 1870–1830,' in Asunción Lavrín (ed.), *Latin American Women* (Westport CT: Greenwood Press).

Childs, Virginia (1985) *Memoirs of Lady Hester Stanhope,* 3 vols. (Austria: Institut für Anglistick und Amerikanistik).

Childs, Virginia (1990) *Lady Hester Stanhope: Queen of the Desert* (London: Weidenfeld and Nicolson).

Conway, Stephen (ed.) (1988) *The Correspondence of Jeremy Bentham, Volume 8, January 1809 to December 1816* (Oxford: Oxford University Press).

Cova, Jesús Antonio (1950) 'Intimidades de don Francisco de Miranda,' *Boletín de la Academia Nacional de Historia*, vol. 33, no. 130 (April–June), pp. 173–81.

Cova, Jesús Antonio (1956) 'Miranda y las mujeres,' *Vida y letras*, vols. 43–44, pp. 43–79.

Darnton, Robert (1996) *The Forbidden Bestsellers of Pre-Revolutionary France* (New York: Harper Collins).

Dinwiddy, J.R. (1975) 'Bentham's Transition to Political Radicalism 1809–1810,' *Journal of the History of Ideas*, vol. 36, no. 4 (October–December).

Duarte, Carlos (1991) *Misión secreta en Puerto Cabello y viaje á Caracas en 1783* (Caracas: Fundación Pampero).

Dupouy, Walter (1945) *Catalina de Miranda* (novela) (Caracas: Tipografía Garrida).

Egea, Antonio (1987) *Francisco de Miranda* (Madrid: Historia 16, Protagonistas de América).

Fernández, David (1972) *La familia de Miranda* (Caracas: Instituto de Investigaciones Mirandinas).

Foner, Philip S. (ed.) (1945) *The Complete Writings of Thomas Paine* (New York: Citadel Press).

Gálvez, Manuel (1946) *Don Francisco de Miranda: el más universal de los americanos* (Buenos Aires: Emece Editores).

García, Lautico (1961) *Francisco de Miranda y el antiguo regimen español* (Caracas: Academia Nacional de la Historia).

González, Eloy (1927) 'Los hijos de Francisco de Miranda,' *Boletín de la Academia Nacional de la Historia*, vol.16, no. 39, pp. 191–8.

Grisanti, Angel (1928) *Miranda y la Emperatriz Catalina la Grande* (Caracas: Empresa Gutenberg).

Grisanti, Angel (1950) *El Precursor Miranda y su familia: primer biografía de la familia Miranda* (Madrid: Talleres Artegráficas).

Hadden, James Cuthbert (1944) *Haydn* (Buenos Aires: Editorial Schapire), colección 'Los Grandes Músicos'.

Halpine, Stuart (2000) *The Altar of Venus: A Biography of Francisco de Miranda* (Bloomington IN: First Books).

Historical Manuscripts Commission (1892–1927) *Dropmore Papers*, 10 vols. (London).

Jacobs, Arthur (1991) *Breve historia de la música occidental* (Caracas: Monte Avila Editores).

Lynch, John (1969) 'British Policy and Spanish America, 1783–1808,' *Journal of Latin American Studies*, vol. 1, no. 1, pp. 1–30.

Madariaga, Isabel de (1950) *Travels of Francisco de Miranda in Russia* (London: [n.p.]).

Madariaga, Isabel de (1981) *Russia in the Age of Catherine the Great* (New Haven, CT: Yale University Press).

Manning, William R. (ed.) (1925) *Diplomatic Correspondence of the United States Concerning the Independence of the Latin American Nations*, 3 vols. (New York: Carnegie Institution).

Mill, James, see William Burke.

Miramón, Alberto (1983) *La llama que no muere* (Caracas: Instituto Panamericano de Geografía e Historia).

Miranda, Francisco de (1927–50) *Archivo del General Miranda* (Caracas: Editorial Sur-América).

Miranda, Francisco de (1928) *The Diary of Francisco de Miranda: Tour of the United States 1783–1784* (New York: Hispanic Society of America).

Miranda, Francisco de (1929) *Archivo del General Miranda*, edited by Don Vicente Dávila (Caracas: Parra León Hermanos, Editorial Sur-América).

Miranda, Francisco de (1929–50) 'Datos a Gennsoné para un Manifiesto sobre la Independencia hispano-americana,' Paris, 10

October 1792, *Archivo del General Miranda* (24 vols., Caracas, Havana), vol. VIII, pp. 8-11.

Miranda, Francisco de (1931) *Fragments from an XVIIIth Century Diary*, edited by Jordan Herbert Stabler (Caracas: Tipografía 'La Nación').

Miranda, Francisco de (1952) *El Colombiano*, prologue by C. Parra-Pérez, bibliographical note by Pedro Grases (Caracas).

Miranda, Francisco de (1959) *Textos sobre la independencia* (Caracas: Academia Nacional de la Historia; Biblioteca 13).

Miranda, Francisco de (1963) *The New Democracy in America: Travels of Francisco de Miranda in the United States 1783–1784*, Judson P. Wood, editor (Norman: University of Oklahoma Press).

Miranda, Francisco de (1982) *América espera* (Caracas: Biblioteca Ayacucho).

Mondolfi, Edgar (ed.) (1992) *Testigos norteamericanos de la expedición de Miranda (Sherman, Smith, Ingersoll)* (Caracas: Monte Avila Editores).

Nucete Sardi, José (1956) *Aventura y tragedia de Don Francisco de Miranda* (Caracas: Editorial González González), fourth edition.

Nucete-Sardi, José (1959) 'Estudio preliminar,' in Francisco de Miranda. *Textos sobre la Independencia* (Caracas: Academia Nacional de la Historia; Biblioteca 13).

Nucete-Sardi, José (1971) *Aventura y tragedia de Francisco de Miranda* (Barcelona: Plaza & Janés).

O'Higgins, Bernardo (1920) *Epistolario O'Higgins 1798-1819* (Madrid: Editorial América), vol. I.

O'Leary, Daniel Florencio (1981) *Memorias del General O'Leary* (Caracas: Ministerio de la Defensa), 2 vols., vol. I.

Paine, Thomas (1945) *The Complete Writings of Thomas Paine*, Philip S. Foner, editor (New York: Citadel Press).

Palacio Fajardo, Manuel (1817) *Outline of the Revolution in Spanish America* (New York: James Eastburn & Co.).

Parra Pérez, Caracciolo (1925) *Miranda et la Révolution Française* (Paris: J. Dumoulin).

Parra Pérez, Caracciolo (ed.) (1927) *Delphine de Custine, belle amie de Miranda* (Paris: Editions Excelsior).

Parra Pérez, Caracciolo (1939) *Historia de la Primera República de Venezuela*, 2 vols. (Caracas: Biblioteca Ayacucho).

Parra Pérez, Caracciolo (1959) *Historia de la Primera República de Venezuela*, 2 vols. (Caracas: Academia Nacional de la Historia; Biblioteca 20).

Pérez Cabrera, José Manuel (1950) *Miranda en Cuba 1780–1783* (La Habana: Academia de la Historia de Cuba).

Pérez Vila, Manuel (1959) 'Miranda en Filadelfia,' *Boletín de la Academia Nacional de Historia de Venezuela*, vol. 42, no. 167 (July-September), pp. 363–4.

Pi Sunyer, Carlos (1978) *Patriotas americanos en Londres* (Caracas: Monte Ávila Editores).

Picón Salas, Mariano (1997) *Miranda*, prologue by Edgardo Mondolfi (Caracas: Monte Avila Latinoamericana).

Polanco Alcántara, Tomás (1996) *Francisco de Miranda. Bosquejo de una biografía ¿Don Juan o Don Quijote?* (Caracas: Editorial Melvin).

Pushkareva, Natalia (1997) *Women in Russian History*, translated by Eve Levin (London: M.E. Sharpe).

Racine, Karen (2003) *Francisco de Miranda: A Transatlantic Life in the Age of Revolution* (Wilmington, DE: Scholarly Resources).

Robbins Landon, H.C. (1978) *Haydn Chronicle and Works: Haydn at Eszterháza, 1766–1790* (London: Thames and Hudson).

Robertson, William Spence (1929) *The Life of Miranda*, 2 vols. (Chapel Hill: University of North Carolina Press).

Robertson, William Spence (1946) *Rise of the Spanish American Republics* (New York: The Free Press).

Robertson, William Spence (1969) *The Life of Miranda* (New York: Cooper Square Publishers), vol. I.

Robertson, William Spence (1982) *La vida de Miranda*, translation by Julio E. Payró. Second edition revised and compiled by Pedro Grases (Caracas: Banco Industrial de Venezuela).

Rodriguez de Alonso, Josefina (1974) *Le siècle des lumières conté par Francisco de Miranda* (Paris: France-Empire).

Rodríguez de Alonso, Josefina (ed.) (1978) *Colombeia* (Caracas: Ediciones de la Presidencia de la República)

Rodríguez, Mario (1994) *'William Burke' and Francisco de Miranda: The Word and Deed in Spanish America's Emancipation* (Lanham, MD: University Press of America).

Romero, Denzil (1983) *La tragedia del Generalísimo* (Caracas Alfadil Editores), Colección Orinoco.

Salcedo-Bastardo, José Luis (1980) *Crisol del americanismo: la casa de Miranda en Londres* (Caracas: Cuadernos Lagoven).

Salcedo-Bastardo, José Luis (1981) *Crucible of Americanism: Miranda's London House* (Caracas: Cuadernos Langoven).

Salcedo-Bastardo, José Luis (1982) 'Bello and the "Symposiums" of Grafton Street,' in John Lynch (ed.), *Andrés Bello: The London Years* (London: The Richmond Publishing Co.).

Ségur, Comte A. de (1825) *Mémoires ou souvenirs et anecdotes par M. Le Comte de Ségur* (Paris: Henri Colburn).

Semple, Robert (1812) *Sketch of the Present State of Caraccas* (London: Robert Baldwin).

Smelser, Marshall (1954) 'George Washington Declines the Part of "El Libertador",' *William and Mary Quarterly*, vol. 11, no. 1 (January), pp. 39–55.

Smith, W.S. (1929) 'Jornal de Prusia, Saxonia, y Austria en el año de 1785,' *Archivo del General Miranda* (Caracas: Editorial Sur-América), vol. I.

Stanhope, Lady Hester (1985) *Memoirs of Lady Hester Stanhope* (Vienna: Institut für Anglistik und Amerikanistik).

Stevenson, Robert (1982) 'Los contactos de Haydn con el Mundo Ibérico,' in *Revista Musical Chilena*, year XXXVI (January–June), no. 157, p. 19.

Thorning, Joseph (1952) *Miranda: World Citizen* (Gainesville: University of Florida Press).

Tromlitz, Johann George (1996) *The Keyed Flute*, translated and edited with an introduction by Ardal Powell (Oxford: Clarendon Press), The Oxford Early Music Series no. 17.

Uslar Pietri, Arturo and Grases, Pedro (1979) *Los libros de Miranda* (Caracas: La Casa del Bello).

Vane, Charles W. (1848-53) *Correspondence, Despatches, and Other Papers of Viscount Castlereagh*, 12 vols. (London: H. Colburn), vol. VII.

Vejarano, Jorge Ricardo (1945) 'La vida fabulosa de Miranda en la corte de Catalina la Grande,' *Revista de América*, vol. 1, pp. 181–98.

Viscardo y Guzman, Juan Pablo (1808) 'Letter to the Spanish Americans,' translated by William Burke, in William Burke, *Additional Reasons for Immediately Emancipating Spanish America* (London), pp. 95-124.

Waddell, D.A.G. (1983) *Gran Bretaña y la Independencia de Venezuela y Colombia* (Caracas: Ministerio de Educación).

Williams, Helen Maria (1827) *Souvenirs de la Révolution Française* (Paris: Dupré).

Williams, Helen Maria (1997) *An Eyewitness Account of the French Revolution by Helen Maria Williams; Letters Continuing a Sketch of the Politics of France*, Jack Fruchtman, editor (New York. Peter Lang Reprints).

Wulf, Karin (1997) 'My Dear Liberty: Quaker Spinsterhood and Female Autonomy in 18th Century Pennsylvania,' in Larry Eldridge (ed.), *Women and Freedom in Early America* (New York: New York University Press), pp. 85–93.

www.ingramcontent.com/pod-product-compliance
Lightning Source LLC
LaVergne TN
LVHW090024310826
846742LV00010B/27
* 9 7 8 1 9 0 0 0 3 9 5 4 3 *